Management of Developing Economies in Transition

Management of Developing Economies in Transition

Choice of Methods and Techniques in Economic Reform

WUU-LONG LIN
and
THOMAS P. CHEN

Westport, Connecticut
London

Library of Congress Cataloging-in-Publication Data

Lin, Wuu-Long.
    Management of developing economies in transition : choice of
methods and techniques in economic reform / Wuu-Long Lin and Thomas
P. Chen.
        p. cm.
    Includes bibliographical references and index.
    ISBN 0–275–94819–6 (alk. paper)
        1. Economic policy. 2. Economic development. 3. Developing
countries—Economic policy. 4. Planning. 5. Finance.
6. Industrial management. 7. Mixed economy. 8. Technology and
state. I. Chen, Thomas P. II. Title.
    HD82.L4746   1996
    338.9—dc20   94–42842

British Library Cataloguing in Publication Data is available.

Library of Congress Catalog Card Number: 94–42842
ISBN: 0–275–94819–6

First published in 1996

Praeger Publishers, 88 Post Road West, Westport, CT 06881
An imprint of Greenwood Publishing Group, Inc.

Printed in the United States of America

The paper used in this book complies with the
Permanent Paper Standard issued by the National
Information Standards Organization (Z39.48–1984).

10 9 8 7 6 5 4 3 2 1

Copyright Acknowledgments

The authors and publisher gratefully acknowledge permission to reprint the following:

Excerpts from *Industry of Free China*, Vol. 77 No. 3, Vol. 77 No. 1, and Vol. 75 No. 6. Used by permission of the Council for Economic Planning and Development, Republic of China.

Excerpts from United Nations material. The views expressed herein are those of the authors and do not necessarily reflect the views of the United Nations.

Table 4.2 from K. T. Li, *The Evolution of Policy Behind Taiwan's Development Success*, Yale University Press, 1988. Used by permission of the author.

Tables and figure from the *World Development Report* 1980, 1985, 1989, 1991, 1992. Copyright © 1980, 1985, 1989, 1991, 1992 by The International Bank for Reconstruction and Development/The World Bank. Reprinted by permission of Oxford University Press.

To Anna, Joel, and Pansy
and
Susan and Wendy

CONTENTS

Contents   ix

ILLUSTRATIONS

PREFACE

Structural transformation in transitional economies and structural adjustment in developing countries have often made headlines over the past few years. Scholars, practitioners, and politicians within the country and abroad as well as international agencies have increasingly focused on the implications of these reforms and the need to ensure their success. In a closely integrated global economy, the success and failure of economic reforms in these countries will affect and be affected by countries of other regions in the world.

In the pursuit of economic reforms, there has been dramatic and nearly universal interest in adopting market principles and mechanisms in hitherto command/administrative economies. Although some countries have made significant progress in terms of rapid economic booming, others have not yet achieved their goals and have even suffered deteriorating economies during the transition period. International experience shows that there is no universal blueprint or model that can meet the need of every country's economic, institutional, and administrative system. Even within the same country, no single system can prevail to accommodate for variations through all regions at different times. This suggests that there must be flexibility in the choice of methods and techniques in economic reform that are appropriate for the prevailing circumstances in each segment of the economy at a given time.

In response to the need for the understanding of diversified experience on economic management, the present book highlights selected development issues of various countries and the international experience. The discussion includes both theoretical insights and a distillation of varied global experience on subjects under the three broad categories of development planning within the framework of market economies, financial management, and enterprise management and transfer and development of technology. The adaptability of these intercountry experiences to a specific situation must take into account the unique features of each country's environment, which includes the impetus for reform, the extent of change contemplated, and the resources and structure of the machinery of government.

The present book was part of a report submitted by the authors to the Development Research Center of the State Council, People's Republic of China. The preparation of the report was financially supported by the United Nations Development Program and administratively managed by the China International Center for Economic and Technical Exchanges. We would like to acknowledge these agencies for the use of part of the report for the present publication. Acknowledgment is also extended to the United Nations, Industry of Free China, who have published earlier versions some of this research, and to K.T.Li, Oxford University Press, and the World Bank for the citation of their published materials. We are indebted to the United Nations for permission to engage in the preparation of this publication outside the organization with which one of the authors is associated. Needless to say, the views presented are those of the authors and not of the organizations and sponsored agencies with which they are associated.

In the course of our researching and writing, we have accumulated many debts to generous colleagues who have inspired and provided guidance on this research, have read chapters, or have otherwise encouraged us: Boxi Li, Huijiong Wang, Gyasi-twum Kwaku, Anthony Bennett, Orlan Buller, Lawrence J. Lau, Pan A. Yotopoulos, Wen Poa Chang, Tzong-shian Yu, and the late Kuo-shu Liang. The authors want to express their appreciation to Flordeliza Manago, Odaris Ithier, Jennifer Wang, and Milena Hama for their typing and research assistance.

Our greatest debt goes to our families for their forbearance and understanding, in particular to Anna Lin for her professional stimulation, and to Wendy Chen for her valuable technical and spiritual support.

Chapter 1

INTRODUCTION

A. BACKGROUND

In recent years, dramatic and far-reaching changes have occurred that profoundly affect the situation facing national economies, and in turn the world economy. One of the most important global trends in world development is the recent transition from a command economy to a market-oriented economy. Other developments include continuing Chinese policies of open economy; the movement toward divestment of public enterprises in many developing countries and developed market economies; and the realization in many countries, particularly in some Latin American and Sub-Saharan African nations, that they have reached the saturation level of their domestic budget deficits, external debts, and servicing obligations.

Economic reform has been successful in terms of economic growth in some countries with an economy in transition. For instance, China has continued to achieve economic booming since 1980s, and Vietnam has begun to achieve a remarkable economic recovery in recent years. However, countries in Eastern Europe and the former Soviet Union as a group suffered from a negative GDP growth rate in the three consecutive years 1990, 1991, and 1992. Such negative economic growth was also observed in many countries of Sub-Saharan Africa, Latin America, and the Caribbean in the 1980s despite their continued efforts in structural adjustment.

Development cannot proceed in a vacuum; there must be a sound macroeconomic foundation. The experience of sluggish economic growth in the 1970s and 1980s indicates that macroeconomic stability is a necessary foundation for sustainable growth. Most governments have now pursued prudent policies in such areas as managing public spending, controlling the rate of inflation, privatizing and managing public enterprises, and developing capital markets. Relatedly, sound fiscal and monetary policies also create a hospitable climate for private investment, thus increasing productivity and generating employment. Moreover, in an interlinkage of the global economy, it is noted that developing countries are also affected by the macroeconomic policies of industrial countries. These include such areas as an adequate supply of external capital (concessional and nonconcessional) and more concession of external debt relief.

The preceding analysis suggests the need for rethinking the role of the state in promoting development planning within the framework of a market economy. Put simply, the government needs to do less in those areas where the market works, and to provide an impetus where the market fails. In other words, the alleged failure of the market in some developing economies may be attributed to the opposite: the ineffective functioning of government interventions in the market.

Government interventions in a market economy are practiced not only in developing countries, but also in developed countries. For instance, during the Great Depression (1930s) in the United States of America, the New Deal program was designed by the federal government to alleviate such specific needs as unemployment insurance, social security, federal insurance for depositors, and government supports for agricultural prices. Also, after World War II, many individuals still survived at a level of poverty and did not enjoy the unprecedented level of prosperity of the nation as a whole. In response to this, President Lyndon B. Johnson declared his "War on Poverty," and a federal program, the "Great Society," was established in the 1960s to assist individuals in such areas as the provision of food, medical care, and jobs.

The role of the government in promoting social and economic development varies greatly across countries according to ideology, political structures, administrative capacity, and level of development. In general, the role of government in social and economic development can be grouped into three broad categories:

(a)   Governments provide certain services that only they can offer, including fiscal and monetary policies and laws and regulations. Whereas the "invisible hand" of the market is adept at operating an economy, the visible hand of government is needed to provide rules for fair competition in that operation.

(b)   Governments have played a major role in providing a whole host of social and economic infrastructure services. These include services related to mass transportation, power, communications, health care, and the alleviation of poverty and illiteracy. Such services are not only humanitarian duties of the government, but also critical stimulants to private sector investment and promotion of economic development. Furthermore, many governments participate directly in productive activities with the aim of protecting consumers from the consequences of market failure. In this regard, government should seek to improve the efficiency of public enterprises through competitive markets.

(c)   Governments often intervene in markets to assume responsibilities that are not easily assumed by individuals, including protection of the environment, national defense, and law and order.

B. OBJECTIVES OF THE BOOK

In the context of global development perspectives, this book focuses on issues related to macroeconomic management in development planning with special reference to international experience in various regions. It includes both theoretical insights and distilled country experience. It is hoped that it will contribute to strengthening the weak link that now exists between planning methodology and planning practice. No attempt will be made here to provide step-by-step guidelines on macroeconomic management. Rather, the aim is to provide support to development planning practitioners in making policies that are appropriate to transitional and developing economies.

The discussion in this book is within the context of the coexistence of development planning and a market economy, that is, a mixed economy. On one hand, it recognizes the need for government interventions through development strategies and policies in order to promote economic development. On the other hand, it suggests that such policy interventions be implemented with the aim of fostering market mechanisms through such measures as provision of externalities and prevention of market imperfection.

Our discussion on macroeconomic management will be based on selected subjects related to industrialization and the market-oriented economy that are part of the emerging themes in both developing and transitional economies. Given the complexity and diversity of these development themes, it is beyond the scope of this book to present a comprehensive or concensus view. Rather, it is hoped that our selected topics on macroeconomic management will provide useful inputs for these development themes.

The discussion that follows includes three parts, with three chapters in each part. These three parts cover broad categories of topics related to development planning, financial management, and enterprise management and technology development.

Part I

DEVELOPMENT PLANNING

A sound macroeconomic foundation provides an important basis for managing a development plan. While promoting the liberalization of the economic system it is equally important to strengthen the role of government in the positive construction of the market mechanism as an economic regulator and a provider of external economies.

Part I consists of three chapters. Chapter 2 gives a brief presentation of intercountry experiences of global development. These are highlights of the successes and failures of macroeconomic development in the past and its future prospects. Chapter 3 presents some guidelines for development planning that provide planners with certain basic information on the management of a development plan. Finally, Chapter 4 discusses the policy framework as a tool for promoting macroeconomic development.

Chapter 2

A BRIEF DESCRIPTION OF RECENT GLOBAL DEVELOPMENT

Although there have been some impressive changes in the lives of people in the developing world in the past three or four decades, the absolute as well as relative disparities between the poor and rich countries have persisted and even widened. These disparities may continue to exist in the foreseeable future. Despite the progress made over the past generation, a World Bank estimate indicates that more than 1 billion people, or about one fifth of the world population, still live in acute poverty. They lack adequate access to such facilities as education, health services, social infrastructures, and financial credit. A new estimate predicts a negligible reduction in poverty in developing countries by the year 2000 and indicates that the numbers of poor will increase at almost the same rate as the population growth in the 1990s.

However, a number of developing countries have deviated from this general pattern, which is based on group averages. These departures from the group averages suggest that in addition to socioeconomic variables, institutional and cultural factors as well as public programs and policies have exerted an important impact on human development.

A. ECONOMIC GROWTH—TRENDS AND LONG-TERM PROSPECTS

Table 2.1 presents statistics on growth of population and output by regions, 1981-1992. The world economy in recent years is continuing in its recovery from the deep recession of the early 1980s.[1] The developed market economies emerged from stagflation and pursued a noninflationary moderate growth path in the last decade. The developed market economies as a group obtained an average annual Gross Domestic Product (GDP) growth rate of 3 percent in 1992. In comparison with North America and Western Europe, developed Asian countries registered the highest GDP growth rate, 4.1 percent, in 1992. However, Eastern Europe and

Table 2.1
Growth of Population and Output by Region, 1981–1992

	Population 1990 (millions)	Population growth rate (annual percentage)	Gross domestic product (billions of 1980 dollars)	Rates of change of gross domestic product (annual percentage)					
				1981–1987	1988	1989	1990[1]	1991[2]	1992[2]
World	5,292	1.8	---	2.6	4.3	3.0	1.0	0.0	2.1
Developed market economies	813	0.6	7,640	2.4	4.3	3.3	2.4	1.4	3.0
North America	276	0.8	2,866	2.8	4.4	2.5	1.0	1.0	3.1
Western Europe	358	0.2	3,467	1.8	3.8	3.4	2.7	1.2	2.3
Developed Asia	144	0.5	1,060	3.8	5.4	4.6	5.0	3.1	4.1
Eastern Europe and the Soviet Union[3]	405	0.6	---	2.7	3.7	1.4	-6.3	-9.5	-4.5
Developing countries	4,074	2.1	2,780	3.0	5.0	3.4	2.9	3.5	5.0
Western Hemisphere	432	2.1	815	1.2	0.8	1.1	-0.7	1.5	3.0
Africa	606	3.1	336	1.2	2.1	3.3	3.4	3.0	3.0
West Asia	130	3.0	357	-1.6	1.1	2.4	0.0	-0.5	7.0
South and East Asia	1,686	2.2	662	5.3	8.7	6.0	6.1	5.5	6.0
China[c]	1,139	1.5	470	10.0	11.3	3.3	4.8	5.5	6.0
Mediterranean	81	1.5	141	3.2	1.4	1.0	-0.7	2.0	4.0
Memorandum items:									
Heavily indebted countries	612	2.3		1.0	1.2	1.5	-0.8	1.5	---
Sub-Saharan[4] Africa	383	3.2		1.4	3.0	2.7	1.9	3.0	---

Source: United Nations, *World Economic Survey 1991*, United Nations publication Sales No. E.91.II.C.1 (1991), p. 10.

[1] Preliminary estimates.
[2] Forecast, based on project LINK and Secretariat estimates. For the groups of developing countries, estimates are rounded to the nearest half percentage point. Eastern Europe and the Soviet Union excludes former German Democratic Republic, which is included in Western Europe; there is therefore a break in the series after 1990 for the developed market economies and Eastern Europe and the Soviet Union.
[3] Net material product: data for 1981-1989 are government estimates.
[4] Excluding Nigeria.

the former Soviet Union continued to register negative economic growth, with a negative economic growth of -4.5 percent in 1992. In the developing world, the annual GDP growth has been increasing, resulting in positive economic growth of 5.0 percent in 1992.

At this point, it is worthwhile noting that there were wide variations in economic performance within developing countries. At one end of the spectrum, many countries, Asian nations in particular, continued to benefit from the global recovery and their economic performance was generally satisfactory. The average annual GDP growth in West Asia was the highest at 7 percent in 1992, representing a magnificent increase from negative growth of -0.5 percent in 1991. However, new economic measures must be taken in order to sustain this level of growth, given the increasing global protectionist sentiment and restrictive adjustment requirements.

In the period 1980-1990, China registered one of the highest economic growth rates in the world: an average annual GDP growth of 9.5 percent. Such rapid progress has been rare elsewhere and is surpassed only by that of Botswana and the Republic of Korea. However, GDP per capita in China at a figure of $370 in 1990 was still low.

At the other extreme, many countries, particularly the heavily indebted countries and those in the Sub-Sahara, continued to face a bleaker future. The average annual GDP growth was only about 1 percent in the highly indebted countries and 1.4 percent in Sub-Saharan Africa during the period 1981-1987. It is noted that the growth of real GDP per capita in some countries was negative because of the high inflation rate in heavily indebted countries and high population growth rate in Sub-Saharan Africa (see Table 2.2). Slackened economic growth was compounded by a combination of factors, including large repayment obligations on existing external debts, deteriorating terms of trade for export commodities, and crop failures.

The long-term prospect for sustained development depends on global conditions and on country policies. The decade of the 1990s may achieve bright prosperity in view of the continued economic reforms and prudent fiscal and monetary policies being pursued by many countries. According to a study by the World Bank (Table 2.2), in the absence of any major adverse shocks and given the pursuit by these countries of good general policies, the projected annual average growth of real GDP per capita for the 1990s could be in the range of 1.8 to 2.5 percent for the industrialized countries, and 2.2 to 2.9 percent for the developing countries. The ranges reflect alternative assumptions about future prospects in world oil price, fiscal deficit of the United States of America, real interest rates, and the trade negotiations under the Uruguay Round.

Within the developing economies, disparities in long-term prospects for economic growth are also reflected in the regional averages. Projected annual growth rate of real GDP per capita in the 1990s ranges from a low of 0.3 to 0.5 percent in Sub-Saharan Africa to a high of 4.2 to 5.3 percent in East Asia. Sub Saharan Africa's growth will improve in comparison with that of the 1980s, but the gain

Table 2.2
Growth of Real GDP per capita, 1965–2000
(average annual percentage change, unless noted)
66 Developing Countries, 1989

	1965-73	1973-80	1980-89	Projection for 1990s
Industrial countries	3.7	2.3	2.3	1.8-2.5
Developing countries	3.9	2.5	1.6	2.2-2.9
Sub-Saharan Africa	2.1	0.4	-1.2	0.3-0.5
East Asia	5.3	4.9	6.2	4.2-5.3
South Asia	1.2	1.7	3.0	2.1-2.6
Europe, Middle Eat, and North Africa	5.8	1.9	0.4	1.4-1.8
Latin America and the Carribean	3.8	2.5	-0.4	1.3-2.0
Developing Countries weighted by population[a]	3.0	2.4	2.9	2.7-3.2

Source: World Bank, *World Development Report 1991,* New York, NY: Oxford University Press (1991), p. 3.

[a]Using population shares as weights, when aggregating GDP growth across countries.

will be small. Asian countries, which account for 65 percent of the population of the developing world, were projected to have a higher economic growth rate than other regions in the 1990s.

B. ECONOMIC GAP AND WIDENING DISPARITIES

Table 2.3 indicates that in 1990, the developing countries as a group comprised 84 percent of the world population and produced 18 percent of the world's gross domestic product. In contrast, the developed high-income economies comprised 16 percent of the world population and produced 82 percent of the world's gross domestic product. In 1990, the gross domestic product per capita of the developing countries was equal to $840, measured in 1990 prices. This figure amounted to about one twenty-third that of the developed high-income economies. In absolute terms, the gap between these two groups was US$18,750 in 1990 prices.

Within the developing countries, disparities also prevail. GDP per capita in 1990 was $110 or less in some countries, such as Mozambique and Tanzania. In contrast, the more industrially advanced developing economies of Hong Kong, Korea, Singapore, and Taiwan, and two newcomers among industrializing nations, Thailand and Malaysia, raised their GDP per capita to a higher level. Some petroleum-exporting countries, such as the United Arab Emirates and Kuwait, had reached the level of the developed countries in terms of GDP per capita.

It appears from Table 2.4 that the absolute gap of GDP per capita between the developing economies and the developed high-income economies was widening substantially from 1980 to 1990. For instance, the gap of GDP per capita expressed in current prices between these two groups was $18,750 in 1990, versus $7,843 in 1980. Put in a different perspective, the GDP per capita in the developing economies as a ratio to that of the developed high-income economies worsened from 1/13 in 1980 to 1/23 in 1990. Although there may exist some statistical discrepancies in these intercountry and interperiod comparisons, such a great difference in per capita GDP would underline the significance of the widening economic disparities between the poor and the rich countries.

Unless the rates of economic growth of the developing countries become much higher than those of the developed high-income economies, it is virtually inevitable that the absolute difference in income will increase, given the initial disparities. Unfortunately, the projected statistics for the 1990s (Table 2.2) indicate that the economic growth rate of the developing countries is not expected to be significantly higher than that of the developed countries. This implies a widening economic gap between these two groups in the current decade.

C. INTERNATIONAL DEVELOPMENT STRATEGIES AND CLIMATE FOR DEVELOPMENT IN THE 1990s

The goals and objectives of the International Development Strategy for the Third United Nations Development Decade of 1980s were for the most part not attained for the following reasons.

(a)   The early years of the 1980s witnessed a recession in many developed market   economies, with high levels of unemployment and inflation.

(b)   Growth rate substantially slowed and even turned negative in the countries of Eastern Europe and the former Soviet Union, where the need for structural transformation became increasingly manifest.

(c)   The decade of the 1980s was characterized by falling economic growth rates, declining living standards, and deepening poverty in most developing countries. It witnessed debt crisis, a negative transfer of net financial resources, and natural and human-caused disasters.

Table 2.3

Distribution of Population and Gross Domestic Product by Major Country Group, Developed and Developing Countries, 1990

Country group	Number of countries	Number (millions) mid-1990	Distribution (%)	Total (US billions) 1990	Distribution (%)	Per capita (US dollar) 1990
		Population		Gross Domestic Product		
1. All countries	125	4,962ª	100	19,469	100	3,924
2. Developing economies	101	4,146	84	3,484	18	840
low-income	(43)	(3,058)	(62)	(1,070)	(6)	(350)
middle-income	(58)	(1,088)	(22)	(2,414)	(12)	(2,200)
				15,985	82	19,590

Source: Tabulated from World Bank, *World Development Report 1992,* New York, NY: Oxford University Press (1992), pp. 218-219.

ª World population is 5.284 billions. Total population for other economies not reported in this table is 322 millions, which is the difference between world population and total population of all countries.

ᵇ High-income economies include Saudi Arabia, Israel, Hong Kong, Singapore, Kuwait, and United Arab Emirates.

In view of these facts, the United Nations General Assembly adopted in December 1990 the International Development Strategy for the Fourth United Nations Development Decade designated from 1 January 1991 to 31 December 2000.[2] The strategy specifies the following four priority aspects:

(a) *Eradication of poverty and hunger:* The goal is to eliminate starvation, famine, and nutritional diseases and to reduce malnutrition and chronic hunger.

(b) *Human resources and institutional development:* Emphasis will be placed on education, health, housing, and employment.

(c) *Population:* Population programs should be integrated with economic goals and strategies. Policies in most countries will focus on reduction of the rate of population growth, an aging population, child care, and woman development.

(d) *Environment.* All countries should take effective action for the protection and enhancement of the environment.[3]

Table 2.4

GDP per capita of Developing Economies as a Ratio of Developed and High-Income Economies, 1980 and 1990

	GDP per Capita		
	Ratio		Absolute gap between two economies (US dollar) current price
Year	Developing economies	Developed and high-income economies	
1980	1	13	7,843
1990	1	23	18,750

Source: Computed from World Bank, *World Development Report,* 1980, and 1992, New York, NY: Oxford University Press (1980, 1992), statistical appendix tables.

Many factors will have an important bearing on the global climate for development in the decade of the 1990s. Table 2.5 presents pessimistic and optimistic scenarios by the World Bank on global prospects. It covers the growth of world trade and finance, policies adopted by the industrial countries, technology, energy, international capital markets, the environment, and security.

No attempt is made here to illustrate item by item the texts contained in Table 2.5, which are self-explanatory. The following observations highlight some emerging issues facing each of the three broad categories of economies, which have a definite potential for affecting world development in the 1990s:

(a) *Developed market economies:* Prudent fiscal and monetary policies are needed in most countries to solve the problems of inflation, unemployment, and budget deficits. In the case of the United States of America and some other countries, consumer expectations and saving rates have been on the low side. Germany and Japan have become the major surplus producers in international trade and investment. Other developments that may have an impact on the long-term economic growth include the integration of the European Community as a single market proposed in 1992, the unification of the former East and West Germany, and the North American Free Trade Agreement of the United States, Mexico, and Canada, which will gradually eliminate duties and barriers on movement of goods and services between the participating countries.

(b) *Economies in transition:* In the transition from a command planning system to a market economy, the East European countries and the former Soviet Union are facing severe disruption of the distribution system and macroeconomic disequilibrium. A number of interrelated policies must

Table 2.5
The Climate for Development in the 1990s

	Pessimistic	Optimistic
World Trade	GATT negotiations collapse; unilateral policies by large industrial countries lead to trade wars; trade declines overall, though by less within regional blocks.	GATT makes real progress; regional GATT – compatible agreements produce dramatically greater integration in Europe, Asia, and the Western Hemisphere; world trade expands rapidly.
Capital flows	International capital markets are overcautious, and transfers to developing countries fail to pick up.	Capital flows to the developing countries resume; greater confidence spurs direct foreign investment.
World Finance	Major institutions fail in Japan and the United States, leading to highrisk premiums, low investment, a prolonged economic slowdown, and possibly higher inflation; the debt crisis continues to impede growth in the developing regions.	Major institutions muddle through; financial reforms and regulatory changes reduce systematic risks; economic recovery is rapid; Brady Initiative and its successors gradually reduce developing-country debt burdens.
Industrial - country policy	Large industrial countries fail to cooperate; they follow poor macroeconomic policies, and financial instability and low growth result.	Macroeconomic policies of the large industrial countries stabilize financial markets and lead to sustained growth.
Security	The decline of the superpowers leads to regional crises and ethnic strife within and among countries; arms races divert economic resources; terrorism, drugs, and poverty undermine internal security.	End of cold war reduces tensions among superpowers; new international security arrangements are developed through a strengthened United Nations.
Technology	Technologies required for competitive products become more and more sophisticated and labor-saving; technology flows are restricted by protectionist policies and firm strategies; developing-country advantages resulting from cheap labor and raw materials diminish.	New technologies improve health and productivity (especially in agriculture); multinationals develop wider global production networks; computers reduce advantages of large markets; better communications make it easier for countries with adequate human capital to catch up in productivity.
Energy	Oil prices remain volatile because of ongoing political and social instability in the Middle East, which continues to be the main supplier of oil.	New political arrangements in the Middle East, combined with a constructive dialogue between producers and consumers of petroleum, lead to a period of unusual stability in real oil prices.
Environment	Damage to the environment mounts with economic repercussions; global resources dwindle; the frequency of local environmental disasters increases.	Environmental ill-effects prove less costly and less immediate than predicted; new national and international policies take adequate steps to protect scarce resources.

Source: World Bank, *World Development Report 1991,* published by Oxford University Press, p. 22.

be adopted. These must include actions in such major areas as price and trade liberalization, privatization of state owned enterprises, modernization of the banking system, and introduction of a capital market.

(c)   *Developing countries:* Generally speaking, Latin America is still battling inflation; Africa is fighting hunger and famine. On the other hand, Asia is continuing its economic boom, in particular the economies of Hong Kong, Korea, Singapore, and Taiwan, as well as Malaysia and Thailand. China will continue to experience on economic boom if it pursues its policies of open economy. In every country, there is a need for continuing economic reform and a clear shift toward policies aimed at increasing the efficiency and competitiveness of the national economies and their close integration with the world economy. External factors that will affect economic prospects in the region include the Uruguay Round of GATT, liberalization policies of developed market economies in the areas of foreign trade, debt relief, transfer and development of science and technology, and external aid and financing.

NOTES

1. Gross domestic product (GDP) as presented in this chapter provides the starting point for the discussion of economic disparities among countries. It measures the total domestic output claimed by the residents.

Alternative methods of measuring worldwide disparities have focused on other measures in terms of energy consumption, life expectancy, and poverty. One study indicates that there exist disparities in quality of life among countries, though of a different magnitude from that of GDP. See United Nations, *World Population Trends and Policies,* chapter 18, "Economic Disparities Associated with Socio-Economic Development," Sales No. E.82.XIII.2 (1982), pp. 227-243.

2. United Nations, *Report of the Ad Hoc Committee of the Whole for the Preparation of the International Development Strategy for the Fourth United Nations Development Decade,* General Assembly Supplement No. 41 (A/45/41) (1991).

3. The United Nation Conference on Environment and Development, also known as the Earth Summit, has been described as the most ambitious undertaking launched by the United Nations. The Summit was held from 3 to 14 June 1992, in Rio de Janeiro, Brazil. One theme of this Summit is the entitlement of human beings to a productive and healthy life in harmony with nature. Proposed programs for environment conservation include a wide range of issues such as protection of the atmosphere and the oceans, combating of deforestation, desertification and drought, and the key role of indigenous people and of women.

Chapter 3

GUIDELINES FOR DEVELOPMENT PLANNING

A. REDEFINING THE ROLE OF GOVERNMENT IN DEVELOPMENT PLANNING

The role of government in development planning is being redefined in the present process of economic transition from a command planning to a market economy and the economic reforms that have been adopted by many countries.[1] Liberalization of the economic system does not imply complete laissez-faire or complete abandonment by the government of all economic roles. What is to be emphasized is the positive restructuring of the market mechanism through the role of government as an economic regulator and a provider of external economies.

The concept of national development planning as a policy tool for the promotion of economic and social development in developing countries has recently attracted growing attention. What is striking about this trend is not simply that the number of countries engaged in development planning has increased considerably; more important, diverse types of planning coupled with a great variety of forms have emerged.[2] There is widespread acceptance of some form of systematic planning for promoting economic and social development, but debate continues over the proper mix and timing of reform measures.

As discussed in this chapter, planning refers primarily to government planning in the context of the mixed market economies of developing countries. Such planning is practiced by preparing and publishing medium-term plans on a periodic basis. Economic development in those countries that practice planning is a process in which planning and direction are intertwined with free enterprise management. The former functions through the direct detailed planning of policy and guidance by a central planning authority, and the latter through the market mechanism as an instrument of plan implementation. This type of planning stands between two extremes: centralized planning, practiced mainly in command planning systems, and indicative planning, followed by several developed market economies.[3] Whereas the former involves detailed planning and mainly uses administered prices, the latter provides only guidelines for economic policies and public expenditures as a means of promoting national economic growth and employment and other related development objectives.

Planning often becomes indispensable in a mixed economy or even a market economy, by complementing the market mechanisms. Many aspects of a market economy lie within the purview of the government, such as the existence of externalities (e.g., monopolies). Planning aids the policymaker in dealing with these aspects of the economy through the examination of trade-offs among alternative policy options. In developing countries, the operation of the market is often imperfect because of the lack of competition or absence of appropriate institutions. In these cases, planning supplements market mechanisms.

Development planning is a complex process, involving many socioeconomic and administrative factors that vary with each country's economic background. Nevertheless, there are common guidelines. This chapter discusses planning in terms of plan formulation, implementation, and evaluation. Although these three essential stages of planning are discussed separately, it should be recognized that they are closely interrelated, with considerable overlap in the activities and responsibilities carried out at various stages. For instance, the formulation of a new plan takes into consideration the results and experience gained from the one that is currently being implemented. The process of plan implementation itself generates information that can be used to modify the current and even the next plan. Plan evaluation contributes to the formulation of a plan by appraising the plan proposal and contributes to plan implementation by monitoring and reviewing its progress.

B. THE INFRASTRUCTURE FOR PLANNING

B.1   Planning Processes

National planning is a systematic effort undertaken by a government to achieve specific economic and social goals. It is a complex process involving many steps. Comprehending the progression through the various stages is crucial for successful formulation and implementation of a development plan. Although in the real world planning activities overlap and interact, it is useful to divide the planning process into five steps for better understanding. These are depicted in Figure 3.1.

(a)   The first input into planning is a combination of economic analysis of facts and value judgments. The facts are the data of the system and may be technical, political, social, demographic, or economic. Value judgments introduce national aspirations or the leader's vision of a country's destiny into the plan. The economic analysis involved in planning refers to causal relationships that determine crucial economic variables. For

Figure 3.1 Steps in Development Planning

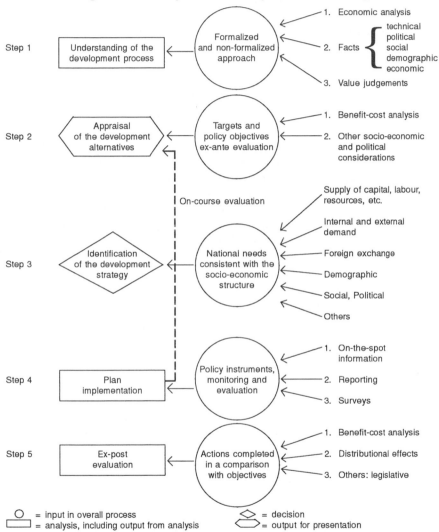

Source: Wuu-Long Lin and MG. Ottaviani-Carra, *A Systems Simulation Approach to Integrated Population and Economic Planning* (Rome: Food and Agriculture Organization of the United Nations, 1975), p. 11.

example, output depends on investment and employment, and demand depends on prices and income. Whereas facts and economic analysis are the province of the technocrats, value judgments are made by the politicians, who represent the common will.

(b)   The second step is a process of formulating alternative sets of targets with crucial economic and social variables and suggesting the trade-offs that may exist among these targets.

(c)   The third step in planning involves identification of the development strategy. To make a feasible and consistent plan, resource constraints such as capital, labor and balance of payments must be considered.

(d)   In step 4, the policy control variables are further specified in terms of policy instruments used in the plan implementation. During the course of implementation, the plan is routinely monitored and evaluated; there is interaction between formulation and implementation. In the case of events that were not anticipated in the plan formulation stage, there must be feedback and referral from step 4 to step 2 to warrant immediate plan modification or revision.

(e)   Finally, step 5—the ex-post evaluation—becomes an important input into the process of learning by doing. The formulation of subsequent plans relies heavily on the experience and results obtained in the process of formulating and executing previous plans.

B.2   Organizations and Participants

The planning system is an interorganizational system involving policy-making, management, operations, review, and evaluation. It is usually rather complex. A simple representation of the basic framework is given in Figure 3.2.

The top level of policymakers mainly comprises senior politicians and administrators. As a group they may be called a planning council, planning commission, or ministerial planning committee. In general, the final authority to approve the development plan rests with the legislative body, whether it is called a parliament or a congress. It is noted, however, that the influential capacity for revising development plans by a legislative body varies greatly among countries.

Whereas political bodies determine broad objectives, set priorities, and allocate the resources available to planners, the execution of plans is undertaken by technical and administrative bodies. A central planning organization (CPO) is often created and made directly responsible to the policymakers. The CPO coordinates and supervises various planning agencies with a supporting staff of researchers and statisticians.

Under the CPO, the preparation of the plan involves the planning sections of various programming and budgeting departments, the treasury, scientific and technological research institutes, and a general economic statistics office. The execution and monitoring of the plan involve various planning bodies, such as the

Figure 3.2 The Planning Framework

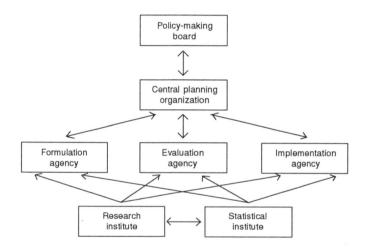

Source: Charles Blitzer, Peter Clark, and Lance Taylor, *Economy-Wide Models and Development Planning* (London, Oxford University Press, 1975), p. 1.

national budget administration, program implementation agency, ministry of public works, and many other national public enterprises, municipalities, and regional development corporations.

A successful development plan requires the participation and support of politicians, civil servants, private sector enterprises, the community, and its citizens, each of which plays a distinct role.

(a) *Politicians:* A national plan is often a political document. The planning period frequently coincides with the term in office of the government, and the politicians use the economic plan as a political manifesto. Planning cannot be completely separated from the political process since it concerns not only economic but also political matters, such as tribal, religious, linguistic, or racial conflicts.

(b) *Planners:* The planners include the technocrats who formulate the plan and the civil servants who implement it. Some are economists or statisticians who compile and interpret data and highlight policy significance; others are experts in crops and livestock, in techniques of the basic industries of the country, in the organization of domestic and world markets, or in coordination with entrepreneurs and trade union leaders.

(c) *Private sector enterprises:* The success of a plan requires the support and participation of the private sector. Resistance from some parts of the private sector will probably be encountered when plans incorporate policy measures that affect their specific interests. Planners should therefore periodically communicate and consult with private sector groups on aspects of the plan that could affect them.

(d) *Community participation:* In a broad sense, community participation involves all the members of a community in the planning, design, and operation of a project designed to benefit that community. One advantage of community-based programs is that they may be less of a financial burden on governments since such programs can be managed by volunteers or regular staff. The communal system in China, instituted after the civil war of 1949, provides a good example of how rural organizational reform can facilitate mass participation in decision making for community development. The commune system made it possible to engage the unemployed and underemployed labor force in agricultural production and rural development, thereby promoting self-sufficiency in food production at that time.

(e) *Ordinary citizens:* A national plan will be meaningful to ordinary citizens and interest groups, such as labor unions and consumer unions, only if they participate in the formulation and execution of the plan that affects them. Public hearings and distribution of plan documents written in simple language for the public are important means for engaging citizen participation in the planning process.

B.3   Data

Planning relies on facts. Statistical information is the foundation of the planning process.

This should include both quantitative information such as the technical aspects of capital/output ratios, and qualitative aspects such as administrative capacities. Generally speaking, basic data for planning include the following categories: national accounts, demography, fiscal and financial data such as revenues and expenditures, technology-oriented information such as input-output matrixes, administration, and management.

Planning without facts[4] is the most challenging task in policy design. Lack of reliable data is a common problem in many developing countries, and particularly acute in remote and rural areas. However, development planning cannot be delayed until all the relevant data become available.

When there is a lack of data, "borrowed" data can play a useful role in development planning. Generally speaking, engineering data such as material requirements of machines and technical coefficients of capital/output ratios are quite stable and can be adapted from other countries. However, behavioral parameters such as price elasticities of consumption and production are more likely to vary among countries to reflect underlying economic differences. Their adaptation from another country's planning must be cautious.

Most planners would agree with Arthur Lewis that "It is better to rely on figures and hunch rather than upon hunch alone."[5] A development plan can be prepared by taking into account deficiencies in the data; then the draft plan can be gradually revised as more reliable data are gathered.

C.   PLAN FORMULATION

A plan is a set of guidelines for development. It defines the government's objectives for the future and allocates resources with due consideration for both objectives and constraints.

C.1   Nature and Scope of a Plan

A development plan may be as simple as a set of public sector projects or as complex as a comprehensive plan for the economy. However, all plans are intertwined. Project appraisal is done with reference to the whole economy, and a comprehensive plan for the economy requires a detailed composition of projects.

(a)   A set of public sector projects are individual specific projects such as irrigation dams and industrial parks. Project appraisal includes benefit and cost, and externalities.

(b)   A plan for the public sector generally consists of two activities. One is social activity, such as education, health, housing, and community facilities. The other is productive activity, such as food production.

(c)   Potential development projects in the private sector must be provided to inspire the plans development. Special attention should be given to the promotion of potential new industries and foreign trade, as well as financial requirements.

(d)   A comprehensive plan for the economy covers the entire economy. All components should be properly coordinated and time-phased to become consistent with the national plan framework.

C.2   The Period of a Plan

A plan period varies from a few months to a number of years.

(a)   A perspective plan usually covers a period of ten to thirty years. Development in certain areas such as preservation of environment and natural resources and interrelated issues of population, labor force, and employment, is inherently a long-term task.

(b)   A medium-term plan covers a period of three to seven years. It usually coincides with the duration of elected officials in the government. It includes detailed plan targets, programs, and policies.

(c)   An annual plan is expressed concretely in terms of planned activities and budget.

(d)   A rolling plan is a revision of the previous fixed plan brought forward to the next plan. It has the advantage of flexibility to revise plan goals in accordance with emerging circumstances.

C.3   Constraints to Development

A development plan must begin with an assessment of bottlenecks in the economy that limit development. Their identification provides a basis for proposing strategies and policies to alleviate these constraints. Constraints vary among countries and generally fall into the following categories:

(a)   Capital formation is the most serious constraint to growth. It includes not only the physical assets of the machine itself but also its technique, design, and administrative management.

(b)   Foreign exchange constraints contribute to sluggish growth in many developing countries insofar as they limit capacities for importing food, energy, science, and technology.

(c)   Land has been the most limiting factor affecting agricultural growth, which constitutes a large proportion of national products and export earnings in most developing countries.

(d)   The fourth major constraint is related to the need for human resources development. A healthy, well-educated population contributes to prosperity and growth. The quality of the labor force improves production. New ideas are generated and actions are taken with regard to investment, innovation, and other opportunities.

(e)   Major constraints to the industrialization of emerging developing countries are the transfer and development of science and technology from developed countries. Adaptation of technology must meet local conditions by considering such factors as rural-based and labor-intensive industries and absorptive capacities.

(f)   In many cases, institutional constraints are a serious barrier to development in the form of shortage of capital or lack of science and technology. These institutional deficiencies may include administrative structures and procedures that place undue emphasis on centralized authority and lack of coordination among government agencies.

C.4   Policy Contents of the Plan

Development strategies are executed by means of development policies. Policies are control instruments that, in fact, constitute specific and operational approaches to the realization of the objectives and the goals of the plan. These subjects will be further elaborated on in the next chapter.

D.   PLAN IMPLEMENTATION

Once the plan has been approved by policymakers, the responsibility for translating the broad targets into concrete projects as well as plan execution rests with the plan implementation agency. Plan implementation is the conversion from a blueprint into action, and the budget is the principal instrument for the translation of plans into reality.

D.1   Conversion of a Plan into a Blueprint for Implementation

Successful plan implementation begins with the plan itself. Clearly, a plan cannot be successfully implemented if it is not realistic, feasible, and specific. Important characteristics of an implementable plan include details of plan targets, specification of instruments used, full utilization of existing capacities, full specification of all project and program activities, consistency and balance, time dimensions, and contingent plans for risk and uncertainty.

Of the characteristices mentioned, the most important is specification of the basic development tasks in some detail so that they can be matched with the planning agencies responsible for their implementation. Three broad categories of plan targets can be identified. One is a sufficient breakdown of growth targets by sectors and industries for use by the ministries and regional bodies in their delegation of functions to various operational units. This ensures better utilization of existing capacities in each sector and industry. Second, aggregative targets must be set for the main macroeconomic variables, such as national products, consumption, investment, exports, and imports. These targets are used to check the internal consistency of the plan in terms of national account balances. Also, the supply of intermediate goods and services, such as raw materials, electrical power, and transport, must be adequate to prevent bottlenecks in plan implementation. Third, policy measures must be specified in such areas as prices and wages, balance of payments, the government budget balance, and employment.

Of equal importance is a full specification of activities designed to achieve specific objectives of detailed projects and programs. Annual budget allocations are made for each project activity.

D.2 Capacity for Implementation

A government's ability to execute development plans and projects depends to a large extent on its administrative capacity and its ability to make adequate budgetary provision for the various activities involved.

The implementation of national plans first requires specific institutional arrangements that identify the functions of public agencies and their administrative units and determine their contribution to economic development. The administrative mechanisms for plan implementation vary considerably from country to country, reflecting such factors as the nature of the plan itself, the stage of development of a country, the nature of the political and economic system, social customs, and cultural backgrounds. Although some of these mechanisms are common to every country, others may be unique to a particular phase of a plan in a given country. In general, administrative mechanisms for plan implementation include political support, central and local level planning agencies, financial institutions, and mobilization of popular support. Promotion of multinational joint action in project implementation is needed when policy areas have an impact across national boundaries in such areas as endemic diseases and flood control.

Successful plan implementation requires proper administration and management. Development experience in many less developed countries indicates that administrative and managerial limitations as well as political instability have been the greatest obstacles to plan implementation. Administrative capability for development is, in its simplest sense, the capacity to mobilize, allocate, and coordinate the actions needed to achieve development objectives. Specifically, strengthening of administrative capability includes such actions as improvement of the quantity and quality of services provided, careful structuring of supervision and support functions, and provision of external support services.

Second, the government budget is an important vehicle for plan implementation. Frequently the main constraints to development planning appear to be lack of funds and poor financial control. The failures of some projects have been attributed to insufficient funds, overcommitment of available financial resources, and poor financial controls. Indeed, the need for plan and budget coordination is critical to the successful implementation of policies and programs. This subject will be further discussed in Sections B and D of Chapter 5 on planning, programming, and budgeting system.

Most governments find it necessary to have an annual budget even though a coherent program requires that budgeting cover a much longer period. The implementation of an annual budget is a crucial activity, partly because it involves fiscal and other measures but also because it is through the budget that governments authorize and control expenditures for the public sector portion of a development plan. Through the annual budget, governments can examine short-run economic impact.

D.3   Review of Implementation

The effective supervision and coordination of plan implementation require the continuing review of progress made toward completion of projects and realization of overall plan targets. The need for such review stems partly from the desire to stimulate the agencies responsible for executing the plan and partly from a need to secure accountability. More important, it seeks to identify the actual state of affairs and the corresponding deviation from planned goals so that appropriate remedial measures can be taken.

Review and management of plan implementation can be classified into the following stages: (1) measurement of results achieved; (2) review of results by comparison with goals of the plan; (3) analysis of variances and identification of their causes; (4) definition of corrective measures; and (5) issue and feedback into the system of corrective measures.

Both review and control of plan implementation depend on an effective reporting system with various checkpoints where continuous comparison can be made between the actual and the planned situation. The sources of information needed range from the project level to the global level, and they may come from routine reports, meetings, and interviews.

Review and evaluation of plan implementation can also be made on an *ad hoc* basis if the existing reporting system is inadequate or ineffective. In either case, there is a need for strong support of political authorities. In some countries, policy and program implementation review institutions are attached to the government. Examples are the Implementation and Coordination Unit (formerly National Operations Room) in the Malaysian Prime Minister's Department, the Operations Room of the Secretariat Information Center in Jordan, and the Regional Review Room in Nepal. In Malaysia, under the personal direction of the deputy prime minister, the status of development programs in each economic sector of all districts is reviewed periodically.

E. PLAN EVALUATION

Several types of evaluation take place in the process of plan formulation and implementation, such as ex-ante evaluation and on-course evaluation.[6] The following analysis will focus on the ex-post evaluation, a systematic assessment of actions completed. It should be noted that the same criteria and methods can be applied in relation to the ex-ante, on-course, and ex-post evaluations.

No plan can anticipate all the uncertainties that may be encountered in the course of implementation. And no planning, however sound, can eliminate all of the difficulties of development in the real world for various reasons, including technical obstacles, changing conditions, or improper use of method and data in plan formulation. Therefore, there is a need for systematic and objective evaluation of plan results in comparison with original goals.

An ex-post evaluation, included as part of the plan from the beginning, tightens discipline among planners and imparts an added sense of responsibility for the successful execution of the plan. It should not simply be viewed as a judgmental act: it should result in improved performance for the next plan.

E.1 Scope of Evaluation

The content and focus of individual plan evaluations may vary greatly. However, although the relative emphases may differ, the following are of concern to most evaluators.[7]

(a) *Effectiveness:* Were the targets achieved? The simplest and least ambitious approach to evaluation is to determine whether the plan has achieved its goals quantitatively and qualitatively. The factors that accounted for success or failure are identified. Conclusions and recommendations are made for the selection and design of future plans.

(b) *Significance:* Did achievement of given objectives contribute to economic development? Development efforts can be measured with regard to their impact on a country and should reflect a society's scale of values or value judgments. It is quite possible that a project may achieve its goal but fail to have any impact on development because the goal was poorly conceived. Similarly, the impact of a plan may go beyond its deliberately formulated objectives and have unpredicted distorting effects on the economy.

(c) *Efficiency:* Was the cost of reaching the targets reasonable? It should be determined whether the program results could have been accomplished at lower cost. Efficiency can be determined by using analytical methods, such as benefit/cost analysis and operations research.

(d) *Compliance:* Were the activities administered in accordance with policies, regulations, and laws? Plan activities should be administered as specified by legislation and regulations applicable to plan implementation. This includes methods of financing its activities, procedures for purchasing equipment, and the nature of any restrictions.

E.2 Evaluation of Public Enterprises

Public enterprises will continue to exist and play a role in the economic and social development of developing and developed countries alike in the foreseeable future, despite the increasing and irreversible trend that policies toward structural reform have had a particular focus on privatization. Greater emphasis has been placed on evaluation of public enterprises since taxpayers bear the burden of losses from public enterprises.

The evaluation of public enterprise performance can be disaggregated into the three elements of financial efficiency, productive efficiency, and response to social goals.

(a) *Financial efficiency:* The achievement of financial surplus is a matter of vital concern to the survival and growth of public enterprises. The absence of adequate returns and, indeed, deficits and losses of public enterprises are causes for grave concern, since such losses will in turn result in subventions and subsidies, a burden to be shared by the taxpayer.

(b) *Productive efficiency:* Although financial profitability is important, it does not provide an adequate measure of the efficiency of a public enterprise, partly because of market imperfections and other intervening governmental factors. It is therefore important to measure productive and technical efficiency in terms of physical parameters and input/output ratios. This includes assessing the optimum use of scarce national resources, measuring the percentage use of capacity in the case of fixed capital, and measuring labor productivity.

(c) *Social performance:* While recognizing the need to measure financial and physical efficiency, it is equally important to assess the success of public enterprises in meeting social goals. This includes public interests in such areas as transportation, human resources development, and environmental protection. One critical question about social performance is how to make an adequate measurement of social goals. Such goals are potentially quantifiable, but qualitative considerations and their assessment remain open to debate.

It is noted, however, that though it is possible to structure independent sets of criteria to adjudicate financial, productive, and social performance, a major question remains on how to interlink these diverse criteria and how to create a composite indicator of performance.

E.3   Problems of Measurement

Problems encountered in the evaluation of public enterprise performance are equally applicable to the evaluation of development plans in general. First, development objectives are usually so diverse that no single yardstick can be entirely relevant to the assessment of all development objectives. Some public enterprises are oriented beyond economic efficiency to include such areas as employment generation, food security, income distribution, and environment protection. For instance, fertilizer may be sold at a low price as a result of government policy to subsidize farmers and to secure food self-sufficiency. Similarly, a plant may receive underpriced electricity and gas as a result of a government policy of protecting an infant industry. Given the complexity of multiple development objectives, quantification is not an easy task.

Second, the widespread lack of reliable information in developing countries is a severe handicap to plan evaluation. Moreover, different intepretations of data can lead to different appraisals of plan performance.

One serious problem inherent in measurement is that the market prices used for planning are not always the same as the social optimum required to guide planning. Market prices are distorted by monopoly power, government administered prices, policies on taxes and subsidies, minimum wage legislation, and maximum price controls.

To correct the imperfection of market prices, shadow prices or accounting prices, which reflect the value of inputs and outputs to the country by taking into consideration non-economic costs and the social importance of development goals, are generally adopted. Measurement of social prices can be a formidable task, involving considerable investigative analytical talent and data requirements. However, some estimations can be based on commonsense considerations of the economy. For instance, zero can be assigned as the shadow price for unskilled labor in a labor surplus economy, and world market prices can be adopted as a weighting factor to approximate the "actual" national prices of those commodities that appear to be protected by import duties or quantitative restrictions.

F.   RECONNAISSANCE OF PLANNING EXERCISES

The four more industrially advanced developing economies of Hong Kong, Korea, Singapore, and Taiwan have a good claim to be ranked as the most successful of the developing economies since the 1950s.[8] With the exception of Hong

Table 3.1
Plan Agencies and Main Nature of Development Plans, 1953–1995, Taiwan

Plan Agencies	Main Nature of Development Plans
In 1953, Economic Stabilization Board (ESB) was established.	The first two of the four-year plans for 1953-60 were mostly on commodity balance and projects and programmes which provided useful references to aid authorities for external economic assistance, specifically the US aid.
In 1958, ESB was disbanded and Council for US Aid (CUSA) expanded.	In the absence of a central planning mechanism, and the Third Four-Year Plan (1961-64) was produced by a coordinating committee. The plan was overshadowed by economic reform in which this Third Plan incorporated the Nineteen-Point Program of Economic and Fiscal Reform, including the trade and exchange rate reforms.
In 1963, CUSA was reorganized into the Council for International Econimic Cooperation and Development (CIECD).	CIECD absorbed various decentralized groups in the past and formulated the Fourth and Fifth Four-Year Plan(1965-1972). Its role was more that of policy coordination than overall comprehensive planning.
In 1973, CIED was reorganized into Economic Planning Council (EPC).	The Sixth Four-Year Plan (1973-76) was a move toward decentralization, and incorporated "Ten Major Projects" and sectoral plans. Subsequently, the Seventh Plan expanded to cover six years (1976-81). Its core consists of the macroeconomic planning, sectoral programme and individual projects.
In 1977, EPC was reorganized into Council for Economic and Development Planning	The 10-year projection (1980-89) was announced in 1980. Development plan reverted to a four-year period, including the Eighth Four-Year Plan (1982-85), Ninth Plan (1986-89) and Tenth Medium-ment (CEPD). Term Economic Development Plan (1990-93). The "Fourteen Key Infrastructural Projects" were in implementation. In 1986, prospectives of the Taiwan economy were analyzed up to the year 2000. The Tenth Four-Year Plan was terminated and the new development plan expanded to cover six years (1991-95). The plan is a forward-looking blueprint for national development, and it is a rolling plan in the sense that major construction projects, if not completed within this plan period, will be rolled into the next plan.

Kong, all the governments have played a considerable role in promoting and guiding economic advance. In particular, Taiwan and Korea, which often see Japan as a model, have had visible state intervention in and effective facilitation of promoting economic development. In Taiwan, development plans have evolved from a simple method of commodity balances and project and sector programs to more complex macroeconomic projections. None of these plans can be regarded as comprehensive planning of the whole economy until the mid-1970s. Rather, government played a role as a coordinating body and the provider of policy guidance.

Table 3.1 presents a sketch of evolution of the planning agencies and contrasting natures of development plans. The following is intended only to give a brief presentation of the nature of development plans in Taiwan. No attempt is made here to describe the objectives and content of these development plans.

Development planning in Taiwan has operated under the framework of a mixed economy. A variety of market-related policy instruments have been adopted to enforce market competition and to inspire individual incentive and enterpreneurship.

As in Japan, Korea, and Singapore, in Taiwan strong government support has made it possible to implement policies smoothly. Whether or not government intervention by means of market-related policy instruments contributed to economic growth is a challenging question since there is no other counterfactual (that is, no policy instrument) with which to compare it. However, one indisputable observation is that strong government leadership has been able to push through several policy changes, for instance, devaluation (Taiwan and Korea), land reform (Taiwan and Korea), deflationary monetary policy to control inflation (Taiwan), encouragement of mass foreign investment (Taiwan and Singapore), and promotion of high-technology industry (Japan, Korea, and Taiwan).

In Taiwan, various development plans contained no binding force for direct government intervention in plan implementation. Even in the public sector, public investment has been decided as part of the annual budget process, but not directly in relation to development plans until the early 1980s. In this regard, the degree of planning in Taiwan is probably less than in Korea and Japan. The Economic Planning Board in Korea controls the budget, and similarly the Ministry of International Trade and Industry has administrative and financial instruments to implement policies on industrial development it promotes. This is in contrast to the Council for Economic and Planning Development in Taiwan, which is not entrusted with enforcement authority for plan implementation.

NOTES

1. The major reference used in the preparation of this chapter is *United Nations Guidelines for Development Planning*, United Nations publication sales No. E.87.II.H.1 (1987). This report was drafted by Wuu-Long Lin for a United Nations publication.

2. The diverse forms of planning include the following: wartime planning, with central control over economic activities similar to those found in a command planning system; physical planning for town and rural areas; anticyclical planning for maintaining economic stability; city and regional planning for ensuring the best possible use of local resources and reducing economic disparities among the regions in a country; national planning dealing with the welfare of the whole nation; and multinational planning, which extends beyond the boundaries of one country to integrate targets for the economies of several countries. See Albert Waterston, *Development Planning—Lessons of Experience* (Baltimore: The Johns Hopkins University Press, 1982), chapter 2.

3. Indicative planning originated in France and is being adopted by such developed market economies as Japan, the Netherlands, and Sweden. State intervention in a market economy makes it possible to assure that private and public sector investment and output plans are well coordinated. Decision making remains decentralized, but the sectors of the economy are guided to meet planned targets.

4. By using experience gained from Nigeria, Stolper systematically discusses how one might deal with actual problems of development planning when time and information are limited. This book helps practitioners prepare a development program for a country lacking the statistical and other information normally required for that exercise. See Wolfgang F. Stolper, *Planning Without Facts; Lessons in Resource Allocation from Nigeria's Development* (Cambridge, Mass.: Harvard University Press, 1966).

5. See W. Arthur Lewis, *Theory of Economic Growth* (George Allen and Irwin, Ltd 1955), pp. 389-390.

6. Ex-ante evaluation is often referred to as a feasibility study, an appraisal of development plan proposals to determine the comparative merits of different courses of action. It provides a basis for policy-making in the light of established criteria, such as relevance to the development objectives, operational feasibility, and benefit/cost studies.

On-course evaluation refers to the monitoring and review of the progress of plan implementation by comparing actual results with planned targets and objectives. It is used for maintaining operational control and revising or modifying all or part of the planning targets.

7. See Organization for Economic Cooperation and Development, *The Evaluation of Technical Assistance* (Paris, 1969), p. 84.

8. For an assessment of the nature and planning exercises in Taiwan, see Ian M.D. Little, "An Economic Reconnaissance," in Walter Galenson, ed., *Economic Growth and Structural Change in Taiwan* (Ithaca, N.Y.: Cornell University Press, 1979), chapter 7.

Chapter 4

AN OVERVIEW OF POLICY FRAMEWORK

Strategies set the development paths; policies place the instruments on a course to achievement of development objectives.[1] A development strategy generally remains the same during a plan period, whereas a variety of policy instruments will evolve to execute this same strategy in accordance with changes in development conditions. For instance, to promote industrialization, the policy instruments used can place emphasis first on import substitution through such policies as devaluation of currency and high tariffs for the protection of infant industries, and then on export promotion through such policies as export subsidies and establishment of industrial parks for promoting high-tech industries.

A. ROLE OF POLICY IN THE ACHIEVEMENT OF DEVELOPMENT OBJECTIVES

Development policy plays four principal roles in the achievement of plan objectives:[2]

(a) *Creation of general conditions favorable to development:* An economy must be characterized by certain basic conditions in order to promote economic development. Development experiences in Korea, Singapore, and Taiwan indicate that stable government, strong government leadership, and sound public institutes are necessary for mobilizing national forces to strive for development goals. There must also be government activities to maintain law and order and stable social conditions, creating favorable circumstances for attracting investment and augmenting production.

(b) *Awareness of development potential and advantages:* The inclusion of policy variables provides the decision maker, the business community, and the public with an opportunity to trace and quantify their impact on development potentials. Before their implementation in the real world, alternative development policies are evaluated and assessed with respect to their effects on development variables, including production, prices, trade, living standards, and economic disparities.

(c)   *Provisions of infrastructures:* Government policies should attach importance to enlarged infrastructure: physical infrastructure, such as electric power and transportation facilities, and social infrastructure, such as basic training and education. Usually, such investments cannot all be made by private individuals, since their benefits spread through the community and do not readily take the form of income to the investor.

(d)   *Stimulation of private activities:* Government policy should be designed to assist private enterprise. An example is the offer of favorable low-interest loans through either government sources or foreign aid. Furthermore, major policy measures should be designed to provide incentives to induce the development of industry. This may include a wide range of measures, such as tax exemptions, rebates of customs duties, and promotion of export-processing zones.

B. POLICY FORMULATION PROCEDURES

The procedure for formulating development policies can be divided into four steps: (1) setting up policy goals; (2) appraising possible consequences; (3) revising policy, if necessary; and (4) selecting a final policy package. These steps are illustrated in Figure 4.1 and are summarized in the following:

Step 1: A combination of the values of the policy variables is set, which includes the change desired by the policymaker. In general, the central planning agency plays an important role in coordinating these targets and their instruments.

Step 2: Information is gathered and processed. Planning techniques are used to ascertain and quantify the effects of policy variables and objectives.

Step 3: Forecasts and projections are made to assess the consequences of the proposed policy changes on national income, employment, prices, and other variables in the country concerned. Alternative policies are evaluated to determine their trade-offs.

Step 4: Knowing the possible trade-offs between policy instruments and targets, the policymaker is able to select the policy packages that most closely approximate the objectives of the plan. If the policymaker is satisfied with the correspondence between policy packages and plan objectives, the policy formation procedure is finished. Otherwise, the policymaker must proceed to step 5.

Figure 4.1   Policy Simulation

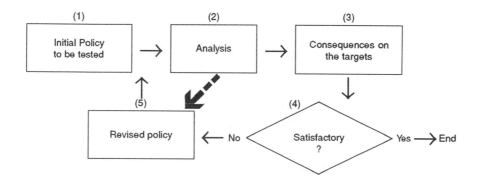

The dotted arrow from (2) to (5) illustrates that the revision of policy is helped by understanding how the sector reacts to each policy instrument.

Source: Wuu-Long Lin and M. G. Ottaviani-Carra, *A Systems Simulation Approach to Integrated Population and Economic Planning* (Rome: Food and Agriculture Organization of the United Nations, 1975), p. 12.

Step 5: The plan's objectives are revised because the original ones appear unfeasible or too costly in terms of trade-offs. The policymaker must then proceed to step 2.

C. POLICY CONSISTENCY

Economic policies must be considered as a coherent whole. Policy consistency is achieved through policy means and aims, decision making among various planning agencies, sectoral balances, time dimension of planned targets, and regional development.

(a) *Policy means and aims:* An important aspect of policy formulation is judging the consistency of aims, and of aims and means taken together. Policymakers are often confronted with conflicting goals. A compromise must therefore be made to ensure the consistency of these different development goals. For example, given resource constraints, policy design should not encourage mass consumption, to prevent reduction of resources for investment at a given time. Attention should also be given to the possibility that certain means may be inconsistent with a given set of aims, or that long-term effects may be unfavorable to the aims. An increase in minimum wage, for example, may improve the income of unskilled labor, but if the increase is too steep, it may endanger future employment and even adversely affect the distribution of income at some later period.

(b) *Decision making among various planning agencies:* In a decentralized decision-making process, the various planning agencies, including the plan formulator, plan implementer, and budget executor, must be coordinated to facilitate the achievement of common development goals. For example, a certain degree of coordination for the objective of export promotion must exist among various institutions responsible for foreign trade, financial credit, science and technology, education and labor force, and energy so that they are consistent with the objective of the national plan.

(c) *Sectoral balances:* Consistency in development planning and programming is usually expressed in terms of economically or technologically feasible relationships between sectors and national aggregates. One aspect is expressed in terms of physical balance, such as a balance of investment requirements and output or an interindustry commodity balance. The other aspect is expressed in terms of financial balance, such as balance of demand for capital and supply of savings, and supply of and demand for foreign exchange.

(d) *The time dimension of planned targets:* To fulfill the overall objectives of a plan, certain policy actions must be taken simultaneously, and others must follow one another in a prescribed sequence. Attention should be given to any possible inconsistencies between short-term and long-term policies or targets. For example, it may be desirable to raise taxes to increase employment in the short term, especially in the public service sector during a boom period, whereas at the same time, it may be beneficial to lower taxes to stimulate long-term development.

(e) *Regional development:* Regional planning is extremely important for geographically large and culturally diverse countries. Regions differ in their natural environment and resources and therefore offer different investment potential. In a multiregional economy practicing either centralized or decentralized planning, policy formulation must deal with investment allocations among regions and the required facilities for interregional commodity flows. The objective here is to achieve balanced regional development with efficient resource allocation and production patterns among regions.

D. POLICY INSTRUMENTS AND POLICY TARGETS

Economic policy is needed in the deliberate manipulation of a number of instruments to achieve certain aims. For example, public work programs may be introduced to provide additional employment, and a land reform program may be launched to stimulate agriculture and food production and to reduce the urban-rural economic disparities. There are thus two elements in development policy, policy targets and policy instruments, to be discussed later.

Planning targets are the aims of an economic policy. Most important among plan targets desired by governments are an increase in real income and expenditure per capita; full employment; improvement of economic distribution among social groups; provision of such basic needs as food, housing, education, and health; and conservation of national resources and environmental protection. In addition, planning targets include the variables required to achieve equilibrium. These are not elements of well-being but rather the foundation of sound policy. The most important examples are the reduction of balance-of-payments deficits, job mobility, and social stability.

Policy instruments are the variables used by governments to reach plan targets. Table 4.1 presents a list of policy instruments and their corresponding impacts on policy target variables. The list of policy areas is not exhaustive, but the aim here is to illustrate the nature of policy responses.

Policy instruments as presented in Table 4.1 are cross-classified in general versus specific aspects, and price variables versus quantity variables.

The general instruments act on broad aspects of the whole economy. These include such variables as money supply and government budget, which in turn impact on interest rates, inflation, and taxpayer burden of the whole economy.

The specific instruments focus on specific segments of the economy. The need

Table 4.1
Classification of Policy Instruments

	General			
	PRICE VARIABLES		**QUANTITY VARIABLES**	
Area of policy	**Instrument**	**Variables affected a/**	**Instrument**	**Variables affected**
Monetary	Interest Rate	(1) Level of Investment (2) Cost of production	Open market operations	(1) Money supply (2) Prices
Fiscal	Personal income tax Corporate income tax	(1) Consumption and saving (1) Profits (2) Investment	Government expenditure	(1) National income (2) Price Level
Foreign trade	Exchange rate General tariff level	(1) Cost of imports (2) Price of exports (3) Balance of payments	Exchange auctions	Exchange rates
Foreign investment	Taxes on foreign profits	Level of foreign investment	Foreign loans and grants	(1) Investment resources (2) Exchange supply
Consumption	General sales tax	Consumption	Social insurance, relief, other transfers	(1) Consumption (2) Income distribution
Labour	Wage rates	(1) Labour cost (2) Profits and investment (3) Labour income	Emigration and immigration	Labour supply
Production	Taxes and subsidies Price control	(1) Profits and production (2) Investment	Government production Government research and technical assistance	Level of production Cost of production

Specific

Category	Specific Instrument	Specific Effect	General Instrument	General Effect
Investment	Interest rates Tax exemptions	(1) Profits (2) Investment by sector	capital rationing Restrictions on entry	Level of investment (1) Prices and profits (2) Level of investment
Consumption	Specific sales taxes	Consumption by commodity	Government services (health, education)	(1) Consumption (2) Income distribution
Trade	Export subsidies Tariffs	(1) Price to consumer (2) Profits on domestic production (1) Profits and investment	Import Quotas and prohibitions Exchange controls	(1) Level of imports (2) Domestic prices
Labour	Wage subsidy	(1) Labour cost and use (2) Profits and investment	Labour training	Supply of skilled labour
Natural resources	Taxes and subsidies	(1) Cost of production (2) Rate of exploitation	Surveys, auxiliary investment, etc.	Rate of devlopment

Source: Hollis B. Chenery, "Development and Programmes," Economic Bulletin for Latin America, vol. 3 (March 1968), pp. 55–60.

a/ All taxes affect Government revenue and saving in addition to the variables cited.

for specific instruments to supplement general measures is due to deficiencies in the price mechanism in affecting certain sectors. For instance, government subsidies and tariffs are generally adopted to promote external trade if the domestic market is at a comparative disadvantage in relation to competition in foreign markets.

Price instruments include variables such as taxes and subsidies. Generally speaking, they impart less distortion to the allocative system of the economy than quantitative restrictions and thus are conducive to greater overall economic efficiency. Also, administrative requirements for price instruments are generally less than for quantitative controls.

Quantitative controls include such measures as quotas and rations. Quantitative measures may be needed in some specific situations such as shortage of an essential consumption commodity and a minimum threshold level of infrastructure, as in the case of power and transport.

E. POLICY EVOLUTION IN TAIWAN

Policy design should take into account development conditions.[3] Correspondingly, policies evolve as economic development proceeds. In the case of Taiwan, as the economy has been transformed after the termination of Japanese colonization, through import substitution, to export promotion, to the present stage of promotion of high-tech industries, there has been a corresponding response in the evolution of economic policies.

Table 4.2 presents a policy matrix for the Taiwan economy, 1950-1985. The policy evaluation chart is cross-classified by three development stages versus ten policy-related areas. The three development stages are classified in accordance with industrialization strategies. These three stages are (1) the import-substitution period, 1950-1961; (2) the export-orientation period, 1962-1980; and (3) the science and technology orientation period 1980-1985. The ten policy-related areas are (1) fiscal taxation on domestic economy, (2) fiscal taxation on external trade, (3) interest rate, (4) foreign exchange rate, (5) international capital movement, (6) government enterprises and national construction, (7) agricultural policy, (8) labor force and labor policies, (9) development of science and technology, and (10) economic development planning.

The table presents the evolution of various policies adopted in each of nine development plans (see also Table 3.1). The following discussion is intended to highlight some major policy issues associated with development conditions and to contrast these different policies during different development stages. Some recent developments of policy evolution since the late 1980s and the new Six-Year National Development Plan, which are not indicated in the table, will also be selectively discussed in the following.

Table 4.2
Policy Matrix for Taiwan Economy

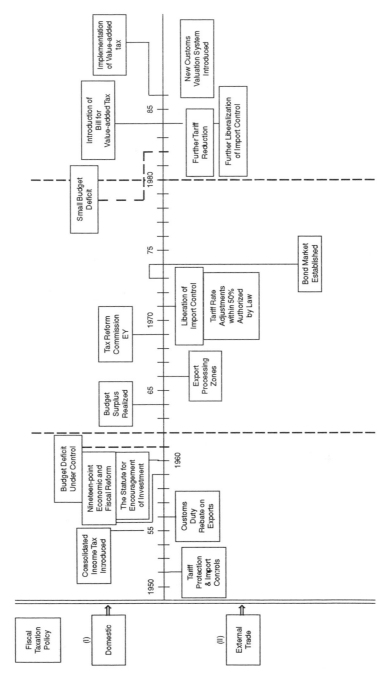

Table 4.2
Policy Matrix for Taiwan Economy *(Continued)*

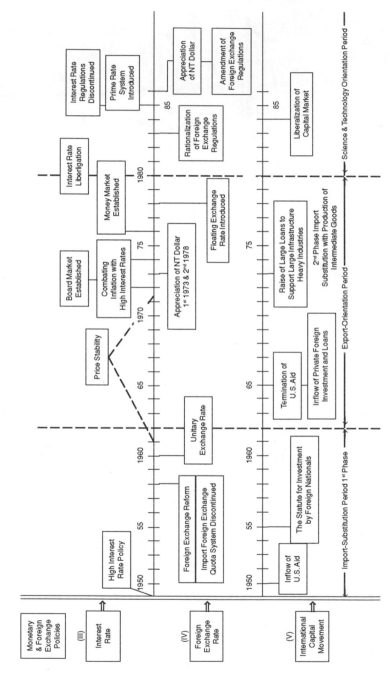

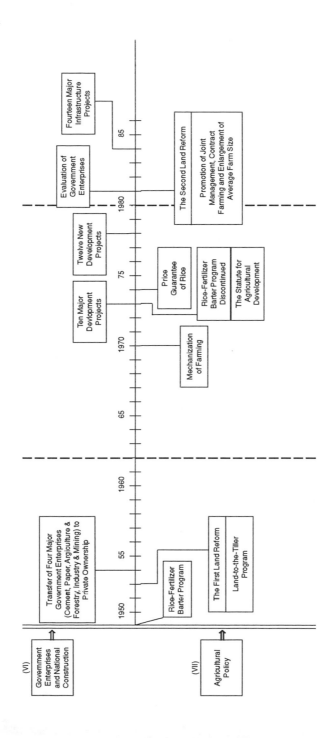

Table 4.2
Policy Matrix for Taiwan Economy *(Continued)*

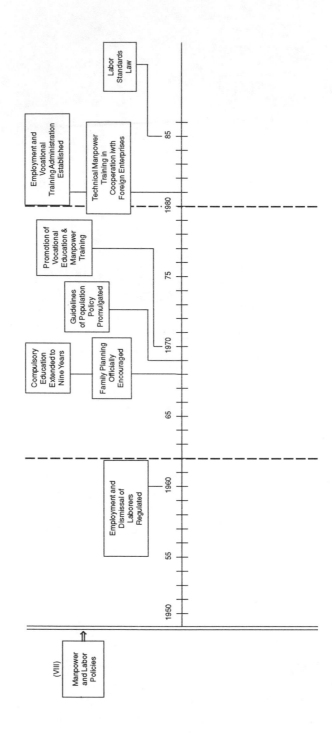

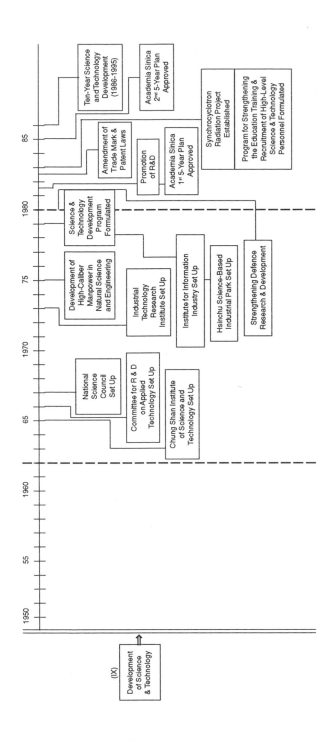

Table 4.2
Policy Matrix for Taiwan Economy *(Continued)*

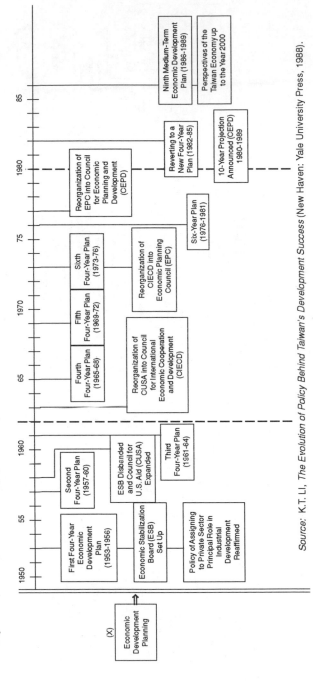

Source: K.T. LI, *The Evolution of Policy Behind Taiwan's Development Success* (New Haven: Yale University Press, 1988).

E.1 Import-Substitution Period, 1950-1961

The approach to the development of the Taiwanese economy during the period 1950-1961 was by way of "nourishing industry with agriculture; and strengthening agriculture with industry." Three policy areas deserve particular recognition, namely land reform, infant industry protection, and inflation control.

(1)   *Land reform:* First of all, a highly successful Land-to-the Tiller program was introduced in 1949. It was carried out in three steps: reduction of farm rent to 37.5 percent, based on the historical yield of the main crop; sale of public lands to tenants; and resale of lands to tenants through government purchase from landlords.

Farmers' incentive to work was strengthened. Correspondingly, there was a rapid increase in agricultural production, not only to satisfy domestic needs, but to export abroad for foreign exchange earnings. The latter was then used to purchase the capital goods required by the import-substituting industries.

At the same time, the fertilizer-rice barter system was introduced. On the one hand, adequate chemical fertilizers as well as other agricultural inputs were supplied to increase agricultural productivity. On the other hand, the barter system with a price distortion in favor of the industrial sector was one of the important policy instruments to siphon off agricultural surpluses, which were used to protect the establishment of a domestic fertilizer industry.

(2)   *Import substitution through high protective tariff and import control:* Taiwan adopted a high protective tariff as well as import quantity controls in 1952 as part of its import-substitution strategy. To protect industries in their infancy, it also resorted to other policy measures, including a system of multiple foreign exchange rates favoring essential imports and credit assistance by the government.

The industries under protection were mostly related to agricultural processing and small-scale, labor-intensive, import-substituting industries. Among them were textiles, food products, fertilizer, cement, home appliances, plywood, and plate glass. These are to meet the need for food, clothing, and shelter.

(3)   *Inflation control:* Several monetary and fiscal reform policies, coupled with the help of foreign aid from the United States, made it possible to control inflation by the late 1950s. From the very start, a high-interest-rate policy was maintained as a way not only to control inflation but to promote saving.

In the pursuit of self-sustaining growth during this period, two important contributory factors must also be recognized. One is Taiwan's colonial heritage from Japan. As a colony of Japan with a food shortage, Taiwan benefited from an effort to increase food production through the buildup of a good network of farmers' organizations and infrastructure, particularly irrigation systems. This laid a favorable foundation for its postwar agricultural modernization.

The other contributing factor is United States aid. Between 1951 and 1965 the United States foreign assistance to Taiwan was over $4 billion in the form of grants, loans, and military equipment. The nonmilitary part of this aid, $1.42 billion, was equivalent to over 6 percent of Taiwan's Gross National Product (GNP). This nonmilitary aid financed some 40 percent of investment and imports during the same period. It also helped the government in its objectives of inflation control, rehabilitation, and expansion of infrastructure.

E.2   Export-Orientation Period, 1962-1979

"Growth with stability" was a distinguished feature of Taiwan's economic development in the 1960s. In that decade, Taiwan enjoyed an average annual GDP growth of 9.6 percent, while consumer prices increased only 3.3 percent annually on average. Taiwan was the first developing economy in the world to achieve both rapid economic growth and price stability simultaneously. In the 1970s, Taiwan continued to enjoy its rapid economic growth with an average annual GDP growth rate of 9.7 percent. But it suffered sharp price inflation, an annual average rate of 10.4 percent, as a result of two world oil crises, the latter of which caused general price inflation worldwide. Comparatively speaking, that inflation rate in Taiwan was higher than that of some industrialized countries, but substantively lower than that of developing countries on average.

Three policy areas during this period are selected here for discussion: export promotion through tariff rebates and creation of export processing zones, the program to increase savings, and the program to promote investment incentives.

(1)   *Export promotion through tariff rebates and creation of export processing zones:* By the late 1950s, Taiwan's small domestic market had become saturated with the products of import-substituting industries, and the official foreign reserves were depleted by heavy imports of capital goods required by the import-substituting industries. To regain its growth momentum, one fiscal policy reform was introduced with emphasis on export promotion.

One policy instrument for encouragement of exports was a tariff rebate system that was first introduced in 1955. This rebate system was operated within the framework of a dual economy. An exporter could buy his imports at world prices because indirect taxes, including import duties, were rebated. Similarly, the exporter could have an option not to import and instead buy inputs from a domestic producer, who was then entitled to claim the amount of import duty that the exporter would have paid. This arrangement created free trade conditions in which products for export could be manufactured at world competitive prices, and the domestic producer of inputs remained protected, but only at the world competitive market prices.

To promote this export-oriented strategy further, the government introduced legistation for the setting up of an export processing zone in 1966. Manufacturers located in the designated zone could import duty-free goods and equipment without a complicated rebate system, but outputs had to be exported. This export-oriented strategy not only rescued the Taiwan economy from potential stagnation at that time but also contributed to rapid economic growth during the 1960s.

(2)   *Increase in savings:* Taiwan adopted a high interest rate policy in the early 1950s and again in 1973/74 in order to combat inflation. This strategy coupled with a booming economy helped to increase savings significantly. National saving as a ratio of GNP increased from 9.7 percent in 1951-1960 to 19.6 percent and 31.9 percent in 1961-1970 and 1971-1980, respectively.

This saving ratio was lower than the investment ratio during the period 1951-1970, but the former was higher than the latter by 1.4 percentage points during 1971-1980. Taiwan thus became one of the few economies in the world with both high savings and high investment ratios. With the saving ratio exceeding the investment ratio after the 1970s, domestic savings could fully meet investment requirements, enabling the economy to achieve self-sustaining economic growth.

(3)   *Investment incentive program:* The Statute for the Encouragement of Investment, promulgated in 1960, exempted investors from paying corporate income tax for a certain grace period after a new investment project started production. Investment incentives have been targeted mainly at capital- and technology-intensive industries, most of whose production is for export. Eligible industries for these tax incentives changed over time in accordance with structural changes in the beneficiary industries in terms of technology innovation.

Policy measures were also geared toward the encouragement of inflow of private foreign investment and loans. This was particularly important because the U.S. aid was terminated in 1965. In this regard, joint ventures with foreign corporations have since been actively promoted by the government.

Other important policy measures taken during this development period included the following: appreciation of the Taiwan dollar, introduction of a floating foreign exchange rate, discontinuation of the rice-fertilizer barter system, introduction of price guarantee for rice, upgrading of labor force quality, and government provision of infrastructural facilities.

E.3 Science- and Technology-Oriented Period, 1980-Present

Three basic policy guidelines were approved by the Legislative Yuan on 20 May 1984: "liberalization, internationalization, and systematization." They can be briefly interpreted as follows:

(a) *Liberalization:* The government will give full reign to the market mechanism and minimize unnecessary interventions in economic activities.

(b) *Internationalization:* The government will promote the internationalization of local industries and participate in regional and international economic activities and cooperation. Correspondingly, it will minimize barriers to the free movement of capital, commodities, technology, and information.

(c) *Systematization:* A market economy must operate within a rational legislative and institutional framework. It includes the streamlining and rationalizing of laws, regulations, and the tax system, and the modernization of the banking sector. All of them will enable the market mechanism to function properly and effectively in order to promote fair competition and to enhance overall productivity and efficiency.

The following discussion focuses on two selected areas: general policy measures and promotion of science and technology.

(1)   *General policy measures:* The annual trade surplus began to increase sharply from 1983. The accumulated foreign surplus had reached US$87 billion by 1992. In order to reduce the pressure of this mounting trade surplus and to achieve economic liberalization, several policy measures have been adopted. These include a substantial appreciation of the New Taiwan dollar, removal of almost all controls on foreign exchange, slashing of import tariffs, and substantial removal of restrictions on commodity imports. These measures have greatly facilitated overseas investment by local businesses. Meanwhile the domestic markets of the service industries were opened to outside competition, including banking, insurance, marine shipping services, fast food, and supermarket.

Other important policy measures that have been taken and/or are under implementation include the following: privatization of government enterprises; a Second Land Reform aimed at promoting joint farming management, contract farming, and enlargement of average farm size; and legislation and legalization of foreign labor and environmental protection. Fourteen major infrastructural projects have also been implemented. These measures helped promote market competition and efficiency and ushered high-tech industries into the economy.

(2)   *Promotion of science and technology:* As the economy is being transformed from labor-intensive industries to capital- and technology-inten-

sive industries, the government has made a systematic effort to promote science and technology development since the late 1970s. The government designated energy-saving, technology-intensive industries as "strategic" industries and actively promoted their development. These strategic industries included machinery, shipbuilding, electronics, and information.

In 1979, the Hsinchu Science-Based Industrial Park was established to promote high-tech and innovative industries. It has become known as Taiwan's version of Silicon Valley in the United States. In 1986 the Ten-Year Science and Technology Development Plan (1986-1995) was formulated. Correspondingly, several programs have been strengthened in the areas of promotion of research and development, and training and overseas recruitment of high-level professionals in sciences and technology.

Presently, the government is implementing the new Six-Year National Development Plan (1991-1995). It aims at making Taiwan a modern industrialized economy by the turn of the twenty-first century.

E.4   Qualifications on Transferability of Taiwan Policy Measures to Other Developing Economies

Finally, qualifications must be made regarding transferability of the Taiwan policy experience to other developing countries. The policies adopted in Taiwan involve the use of a variety of market-related policy instruments such as money supply growth rate, tax rate, foreign exchange rate, and interest rate. They were used to create profits for domestic import-substituting firms and to create revenue for the government. These creations of firm profits and government revenues were then used to expand facilities for export promotion. This policy evolution for promoting industrialization was operated within a market framework.

Therefore, the policy experience of Taiwan can be easily transferred to the economies of other developing countries where market forces are an important mechanism in motivating individual initiatives and private enterprises. However, the policy experience of Taiwan cannot be easily transferred to a command planned economy where political rules overshadow market forces.

Also, Taiwan policy experience cannot be transferred to other developing countries as a whole package because of different development conditions at a given time. But some individual measures can be easily adopted by other developing countries; these include use of high interest rates for promoting savings, export promotion through subsidies, establishment of export processing zones and industrial parks, and government provision of adequate infrastructure and encouragement of research and development.

However, some other individual measures adopted in Taiwan are not likely to be transferable to other developing countries. For instance, land reform was carried out by government leaders who were evacuated from mainland China and therefore had no vested interest in land ownership in Taiwan. The efficient utilization of the U.S. economic aid was carried out by many experienced professionals who were evacuated from mainland China to Taiwan after World War II. Such extensive trained human resources were not available in Taiwan at that time.

NOTES

1. The major reference for preparing this chapter is *United Nations Guidelines for Development Planning*, United Nations publication sales No. E.87.II.H.1 (1987).

2. See Jan Tinbergen, *The Design of Development* (Baltimore: The Johns Hopkins University Press, 1958).

3. For details see K. T. Li, *The Evolution of Policy Behind Taiwan's Development Success* (New Haven, Conn.: Yale University Press, 1988).

Part II

FINANCIAL MANAGEMENT

In a monetary economy where finance is a vehicle to carry on a development plan, effective financial management is important for promoting economic development. As economic plan is analogous to a human body's muscles, finance is analogous to the blood. One cannot function without the other. Therefore, in order to implement a development plan for achieving its objectives, government financial management is an indispensable tool for mobilizing, allocating, and utilizing resources efficiently and effectively.

The following discussion includes three chapters, namely, Chapter 5 financial management process in government, Chapter 6 changing roles of public sector in financial resources mobilization, and Chapter 7 control and management of public expenditure.

Chapter 5

THE FINANCIAL MANAGEMENT PROCESS IN GOVERNMENT

A. INTRODUCTION

Governments of today have varying priorities, but they all face the same task of discovering the most cost-effective means of achieving their chosen development goals with limited resources.[1] Different governments may adopt different approaches and techniques within their own institutional frameworks, but all have recognized that sound financial management is a crucial factor not only in enforcing accountability to the legislature but, more importantly, in efficiently allocating resources and implementing development plans. Improved systems of budgeting, accounting, and auditing, and their links with each other, are indispensable to the strengthening of financial management and the promotion of social and economic development.

The persistent demand for the improvement of government financial management stems from a wide range of services and activities, involving sizable public funds assumed by governments on behalf of their societies.

As a result of the active and growing role played by governments in developing and developed countries alike (see the preceding discussion of the intensifying role of government in promoting economic development), public expenditure has increased rapidly and become diversified, and public-sector transactions have grown more and more complex. This has given rise to the need for stronger financial management in government. Concern about this subject is particularly keen during the current period of economic austerity, when developing countries face rather dim prospects of obtaining net capital flows from developed market economies. And, given the limited resources of today's complex economic, political, and social environment, government policymakers and authorities are being pressed harder than ever to pay attention to "value for money" considerations.

It is recognized that the various approaches adopted by different countries have resulted in various achievements, illustrating the difficulty of establishing a uniform approach to financial management that can be applied to every country. There must be flexibility in the choice of methods, procedures, and techniques of financial control, to ensure that they are appropriate to each prevailing circumstance.

Despite differences in relative settings, there are factors common to all forms of government financial management. The present chapter aims at giving a bird's-eye view of this subject, with the hope that it will provide useful lessons and insights for developing countries that are seeking to improve their administrative machinery for financial management.

The chapter begins with a brief review of the financial management process in Section B. Section C examines the institutional framework. Some aspects of the integrated process of financial management are examined in Section D. Closing remarks are given in the last section.

B. THE FINANCIAL MANAGEMENT PROCESS

Systems of government financial management differ from country to country in numerous ways.[2] One common characteristic, however, is that they all involve the periodic (usually annual) preparation of budgets. Under the system established by Gladstone in the United Kingdom during the nineteenth century and well known in most countries today, the management cycle generally consists of estimate, appropriation, and audit. But the vast increase in public spending and its diversity in the twentieth century have resulted in the need for supplementation and more sophistication.

The financial management process in most countries today can be conceptually depicted in four broad phases (see Figure 5.1). The process begins with the planning and programming phase, proceeds through the budget formulation and budget execution and accounting phases, and concludes with the audit and evaluation phases, after which the budget cycle begins again.

Briefly stated, plans, programs, and related policies are first formulated for public-sector activities and then implemented through the instrumentality of a government budget. Budgeting takes into account the level of resources and determines their allocation among competing needs to achieve predetermined objectives. Budget execution and accounting translate budget proposals into practice and monitor compliance with preestablished targets. Auditing and evaluation are concerned with the accuracy and reliability of financial information and the efficiency and effectiveness of government transactions. Each of the phases forms a separate, but interdependent part of the financial management process. The phases are presented in Figure 5.1 and are discussed in the following sections.

Figure 5.1
Conceptual Framework of Financial Management Process

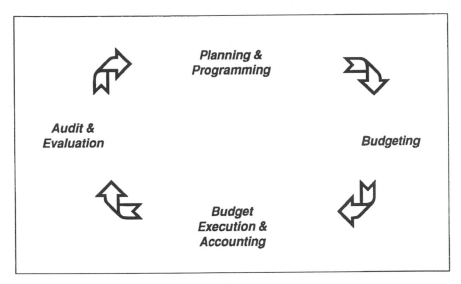

Source: *Managing the Cost of Government-Building an Effective Financial Management Structure,* United States General Accounting Office, GAO/AFMD-85-35-A: Washington, D.C., Government Printing Office (1985), p. 12.

B.1 Planning and Programming

Sound financial management requires careful planning and programming to enable policymakers to focus their policy deliberations more systematically on the nation's development strategies and major issues. Planning represents the strategic element for selecting courses of action by systematic consideration of alternatives with meaningful potential. And programming is the tactical component that employs quantitative analysis to select programs and examine factors such as personnel, materials, and facilities that are necessary for accomplishing program goals.

The widespread adoption of planning and programming stems principally from the view that they make the budgeting process more meaningful. Development objectives and the availability of and relationships among resources are taken into account to achieve a coherent and comprehensive program of action for the nation as a whole. Costs and benefits are considered prior to budget making.

The planning and programming process provides an essential analytical framework for decision making to ensure the selection of realistic goals that can be afforded, given limited resources. It also provides a means of comparing the benefits of past decisions with the actual costs involved, and of applying this experience more effectively for future reference to financial management decision making.

Planning is an important strategic issue in financial management. Without a forward view, financial events that could have been anticipated come unexpectedly. Correspondingly, contingency plans cannot be made and decision making lacks perspective.

In most developing countries, the framework for the preparation of the annual investment and current budgets is the five-year development plan, which is structured under the guidance of a planning commission (e.g., Nepal and Bhutan) or the ministry or department of national development and economic planning (Sierra Leone and Malawi) or the ministry of planning (Bangladesh). Essentially these organizations perform the same functions. This multiyear forward planning provides a basis for preparing budget funds which are usually allocated on an annual basis.

B.2   Budgeting

Government budgeting is the monetary translation of all programs and activities of government within a given period. It involves three different but related tasks related to revenue and expenditures.

On the revenue side, it entails careful and realistic estimation of revenue for the ensuing period based on relevant economic and financial data and the outcomes or results achieved in the preceding budget period. On the expenditure side, it involves exchaustive estimation of expenditure patterns and projections made by various spending units and agencies on the basis of their previous year's experience and their requirements for implementation of ongoing and newly planned programs and projects during the given period. The third aspect of the process is a balancing act concerned with the development of plans and policy initiatives for raising revenue or other funds to meet any resulting resource gap.

Development budget and current budget for project maintenance should be equally emphasized. Projects supported by the development budget are counterproductive unless the recurrent budget provides sufficient funds for their maintenance and operation.

Yet, the tendency in many countries is to underplay the current budget in favor of the development budget. Attempts have been made by many countries to correct the conditions of separate and disjointed decisionmaking on development and current budgets. For instance, Nepal has developed a classification system that covers both development and current expenditures. Somalia has a comprehensive and united budget that includes funding for the central and local governments' investment projects and public enterprises.

B.3   Budget Execution and Accounting

Budget execution is action that translates budget proposals into practice, thus making government policies a reality. Government accounting is an indispensable tool for the effective management and monitoring of budget implementation. The records on receipts, expenditures, and all related activities provide the financial information essential to effective and efficient management of government program operations.

The availability of such data also permits the prompt and accurate determination of costs, benefits/outputs, and productivity. In the absence of adequate reporting systems, accountability to the legislature and satisfactory implementation of programs and projects cannot be assured, nor can financial objectives and the actions of those responsible for budget execution be properly evaluated.

The reporting system should provide information relevant to the functions of control, including cost control, funds control, cash control, revenue control, and debt management.[3]

(a)   *Cost control:* Public monies should be spent in a way that minimizes cost and maximizes return for the resources invested. Cost control means more than the control of spending; it means evaluation of the relationships between the costs and the benefits of government activities. Cost control also means varying the composition of costs and managing costs efficiently in order to achieve value for money with limited resources. Information on the costs and results of previous and current activities provides the basis for decisions concerning future government activities.

(b)   *Fund control:* The object of fund control is to ensure that funds are used appropriately for authorized purposes. Otherwise stated, obligations and disbursements should not exceed the amounts authorized and available. Several techniques may be used to control the allocation and disbursement of funds, including completely impounding appropriations, clamping down on year-end spending sprees, and earmarking parts of appropriations for certain key programs.

(c)   *Cash control:* Cash flow dictates the ability to carry out planned programs. Governments should mobilize cash on hand and pool all the cash in the general or consolidated fund. Cash management requires, among other things, assessment of seasonality of revenues and expenditures, advance information about the pattern and timing of expenditure, forecasts of cash requirements, and investment of idle cash balances.

(d)   *Revenue control:* Revenue control refers to the timely collection of amounts due the central government. In many countries, a national network has been set up to accelerate the flow of receipts. Payers send their remittances to a designated bank or agency, which immediately credits them to the central account of the treasury. Also, various reforms have enabled tax systems to assess and collect taxes more effectively and to cope with tax evasion.

(e) *Debt management:* Related to the varieties of controls discussed previously is the emerging issue of debt management. Debt management involves reducing indebtedness to the minimum amount and cost, by using available resources to the maximum possible extent and thus avoiding borrowing and by using the cheapest terms in relation to the duration and interest rates.

B.4   Audit/Evaluation

Traditionally, post budget evaluation has been undertaken in the form of audits. Evaluation, however, is not limited to government audits, which have traditionally been largely confined to accountability, appropriate audits, and ensuring of financial propriety. The scope of evaluation and auditing has already been discussed in Section E of Chapter 3 on plan evaluation.

A variety of evaluation instruments have been developed, including legislation, regulations, manuals, systems of authorization, and internal checks. Nevertheless, evaluation/auditing cannot achieve its intended objectives. Some of these areas are presented next.

(a) *Financial regulations:* They are outmoded in many countries. The rules are no longer operative or appropriate to present conditions.

(b) *Control of public enterprises:* Public enterprises are often in receipt of government grants/loans, but the ministry of finance often encounters difficulties in their evaluation. Such difficulties include attempts by public enterprises to avoid servicing and repaying loans and poorly substantiated claims for rolling over loans or receiving grants by public enterprises.

(c) *External development budget:* Projects that are financed partly or wholly from external funds are often formulated and proposed through the planning ministry. Although the function of the ministry of finance is to manage the funds, they often lack authority to control external funds.

C.   INSTITUTIONAL MECHANISM

Financial management is an interorganizational system involving the executive branch, policymakers, and various agencies, as well as interest groups and ordinary citizens. The institutional mechanism relating to policy, revenues, and expenditures involves at least four authorities: the executive branch of the government, the ministry of finance, the treasury, and the legislature.

Each country has its own institutional framework. Canada, the United Kingdom, and the United States have been selected to illustrate the institutional framework for the financial management process.[4] The first two countries operate under a parliamentary system, whereas the last has a congressional system. With respect to the two types of legislature, the latter type has more influence on the budgetary process than the former.

C.1   Canada

In Canada, the government budget is prepared and submitted by the executive branch, and its approval by Parliament is largely a matter of form. Parliament could pass a vote of no confidence in the governing party if it wished to reject the executive's spending plans, but this would mean the fall of the government. In practice, this happens only infrequently.

(1)   *Executive branch:* The budget of the government is prepared by the executive branch each year. It is important to recognize from the outset that what is proposed by the executive branch requires the concurrence and understanding of Parliament.

The main estimates are prepared and submitted first and are followed by supplementary estimates, usually in the late fall of each year or just before the end of each fiscal year. The purpose of the supplementary estimates is to finance unanticipated expenditures. However, many new or enriched programs are now primarily financed through supplementary estimates.

There are three central agencies in the executive branch, namely, the Privy Council Office, the Treasury Board, and the Ministry of Finance. Each plays a distinct role in financial management.

(a)   *Privy Council Office (PCO):* PCO is the advisory staff to the prime minister and is the central coordinator and catalyst of policy issues, including financial management and related matters. PCO has a broad perspective and analyzes all policy initiatives that come to the attention of the cabinet.

(b)   *The Treasury Board:* One of the major tasks assigned to the board is the drafting of a "call letter" to each department and agency, requesting the submission of estimates in the form of a multiyear operational plan. Although financial administration of cash disbursements through appropriations approved by Parliament remains an important activity, emphasis is also placed on internal management with the aim of maximizing efficency and effectiveness in the expenditure of public funds.

(c)   *Ministry of Finance:* The Ministry of Finance is primarily responsible for taxation policy and the regulation of financial institutions and markets, as well as the fiscal aspects of federal-provincial relations. On the basis of its projections of major macroeconomic indicators, such as output, population, unemployment, and prices, it estimates the funds available in the future, which should be consistent with economic stabilization policies.

(2) *Parliament:* Each year, the parliament votes on the main and supplementary estimates for each department submitted by the president of the Treasury Board. The so-called supply bills become appropriation acts after they have received Senate approval and Royal Assent. Only then can the funds be spent.

In a legal sense, it is the Parliament that approves the government's budget. In practice, approval of the government's expenditure plans by Parliament is largely pro forma. Under the cabinet-Parliament system of government, there is an all-or-nothing choice put to Parliament by the executive. Parliament can reject the package of government budget plans through a no-confidence vote, which also means the fall of the government. This, however, seldom happens.

C.2 United Kingdom of Great Britain and Northern Ireland

The preparation of the budget lies exclusively within the competence of the executive branch, acting through the Treasury. Each year, after preparation, the budget is submitted to Parliament for approval.

(1) *Executive branch:* The institutional framework of financial management in the United Kingdom can be best explained in relation to the roles played by the chancellor of the Exchequer, the chief secretary to the Treasury, and the spending departments.

(a) *The chancellor of the Exchequer:* The chancellor has enormous power to determine total planned expenditure, subject to the ultimate adjudication of the cabinet. A total spending limit is determined independently rather than through a summation of departmental bids. In proposing a spending limit, the chancellor takes into account not only the amount of spending but also the effects of spending on taxation and macroeconomic growth, unemployment, the money supply, and the balance of payments.

(b) *The chief secretary of the Treasury:* The chief secretary usually has the responsibility of apportioning funds among programs. In the context of the public expenditure committee system, the Treasury screens the spending ministries' estimates and bargains with the ministries over expenditures. It is the responsibility of the executive, acting through the Treasury, to submit the budget to Parliament for approval.

(c) *Spending ministries:* The spending of allocated resources is the responsibility of the respective ministries. The Treasury's power does not extend to the direct supervision of budget implementation, although the Treasury plays the decisive role in budget preparation and collaborates with the external organs of control.

(2)   *Parliament:* In the House of Commons, expenditures and revenues are reviewed separately by the Committee of Supply and the Committee of Ways and Means. Once the resolution has been passed by a vote, appropriations and revenue form the subject of two annual laws—the Appropriation Act and the Finance Act.

The National Audit Office (NAO), headed by the comptroller and auditor-general, exercises external control over public spending at the central government level, although there is also an internal control within the executive branch exercised by the Treasury and the spending departments. NAO is directly responsible to Parliament and prepares an annual audit report of the accounts of each ministry for consideration by the House of Commons.

C.3 United States of America

With regard to legislative influence on public spending, the United States differs markedly from Canada and the United Kingdom. In the United States, to a large extent, Congress can and does frequently modify the expenditure proposals of the executive branch, whereas public spending in Canada and the United Kingdom is firmly controlled by the executive branch.

The budgetary process of the federal government in the United States comprises four distinct administrative and decision-making phases: budget preparation by the Office of Management and Budget, congressional approval and revision of the executive budget, implementation of the appropriation bills by the executive branch, and auditing by the General Accounting Office.

(a)   *The Office of Management and Budget (OMB):* Each year OMB prepares the budget and presents it to Congress for approval. OMB scrutinizes the budget in line with the wishes of the president. Budget preparation is a lengthy process, involving a series of budget hearings and consultations with other agencies, such as the Treasury and the Council of Economic Advisors, regarding tax implications and the impact on the economy.

(b)   *Congress:* Congress appraises and revises the executive budget and passes it by voting in favor of the budget legislation. Reconciliation has come to assume a more permanent and prominent role in congressional budgeting. The Congressional Budget and Impoundment Control Act of 1974 strengthens the position of Congress on budgeting. Under the act, the Congressional Budget Office (CBO) was established to assist Congress in its control of finance. CBO provides an independent assessment of the state of the economy and of national needs, which can be set against that of OMB.

(c)   *Spending agencies:* Once the budget is enacted, it is the responsibility of the executive branch to implement it. The executive branch has some flexibility in timing the implementation. However, the 1974 act restricts the president's ability to impound funds that have been legislated by Congress.

(d)   *General Accounting Office (GAO):* GAO is an independent agency outside the executive branch that is directly responsible to Congress. The major focus of GAO's work is on accounting and auditing of the federal budget programs, activities, and financial operations.

D. SOME CONSIDERATIONS ON THE INTEGRATED PROCESS OF FINANCIAL MANAGEMENT

Weaknesses in government financial management exist in most countries. Recently, the United Nations conducted a study on this subject in six of the least developed countries, Bangladesh, Bhutan, Malawi, Nepal, Sierra Leone, and Somalia. The extent of the weaknesses and their nature differed widely. However, there are some common features[5]:

(a)   In planning their budgets, the spending agencies get only minimal fiscal and policy guidance from the ministries of finance and planning.

(b)   There is lack of coordination between recurrent and development budgets. Frequently, recurrent budgets suffer most during economic austerity.

(c)   Untimely and inaccurate government accounting systems and other information could not provide adequate data for such processes as budget formulation, budgetary control, performance monitoring, financial planning, and formulation of fiscal policies. Most countries require the submission of financial statements and audit reports only a few months after the end of the fiscal year. Yet, not all countries have been able to keep to the established timetables. Sierra Leone, for instance, is currently attempting to resolve a backlog of several years.

(d)   Often the monitoring of budget implementation focuses solely on expenditure control itself with little emphasis on project management and efficiency and effectiveness of expenditures.

(e)   Attempts have been made to computerize government financial information systems, but they have not yielded satisfactory results. Problems encountered include lack of flexibility in batch processing, equipment breakdowns, and inaccuracy of data.

Although some of these weaknesses are related to improper functions and inadequate authorities in the financial management system itself, others are caused by the lack of coordination in the process of financial management. Although it is often useful to distinguish among the phases of planning and programming, budgeting, budget execution, accounting, and audit/evaluation in financial management, there exists a close relationship among them. In practice, these phases cannot be separated. For instance, budget implementation generates information that is useful to the next cycle of budget formulation as well as to the modification of the present one.

The major weakness of the present financial management process, as presented in Figure 5.1, lies in the sequential order upon which the overall process is dependent. There is a lack of interaction and feedback among the processes. Consequently, the results generated by different phases are not effectively used. For instance, whereas the budget is normally prepared on a program and appropriation-account basis, such as dams for flood control, the accounting is generally done on an organization and object-classification basis, such as personnel and purchases of equipment. As a result, actual results achieved cannot be measured meaningfully against plans.

Figure 5.2 presents a conceptual framework of an integrated process of financial management. Information systems, including both organizational structure and computerized information systems, serve as a coordination unit in integrating the independent phases of financial management process.

Some considerations related to an integrated process to strengthen financial management are briefly discussed next in terms of budgeting and planning, classification of budget and accounts at the same basis, accrual accounting, long-term financial survey, and financial-information systems.

D.1 Budgeting and Planning

Development planning and budgeting differ. In particular, the time horizon and scope of the former are wider than those of the latter. However, development planning and budgeting are essentially complementary and companion processes, as long as both are viewed as operational instruments for achieving national development goals.

Coordination between budgeting and planning can be strengthened if the budgetary process corresponds conceptually to the planning process. On the one hand, budgeting should be used as an effective vehicle for the formulation of goals and the mobilization and allocation of resources, and as an instrument for implementation of programs and policies and monitoring and review of performance. The policies and techniques of revenue collection and expenditure appropriation must be closely related to national development tasks. On the other hand, the development plan must be critically examined in the light of financial capacities. One important consideration is internal consistency. This includes not only a physical

Figure 5.2
Conceptual Framework of Integrated Process of Financial Management

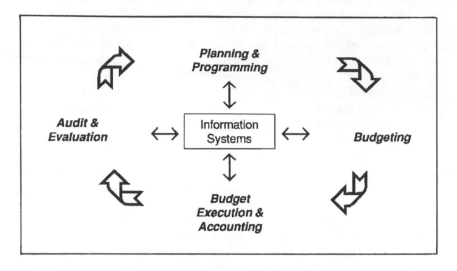

balance, such as that between the demand for and the availability of raw materials and skilled labor, but also a more important economic balance, such as the balance between savings and investment and that between the need for and the availability of foreign exchange.

Conventional practices such as cabinet meetings, interdepartmental consultations, and public hearings continue to provide an invaluable channel for obtaining policy compromises and effectively integrating planning and programming into the financial management process. More recently, a formal and quantitative approach has been introduced via the planning, programming, and budgeting system (PPBS). PPBS rationalizes and systematizes financial management decision making by quantitatively appraising the effectiveness and efficiency of alternative programs and by assessing the expenditures and accomplishments of each program, which may be spread over many years. PPBS may, therefore, be considered a decision model for development planning and budgeting.

Table 5.1 presents an example of budget classification under the PPBS framework. First, it lists the major programs. Then their corresponding functions and organizations are also identified. And for each program, it gives a list of projects required for completing a given program and the units for the measurement of end products. In this illustration, the function of agriculture, for example, can be carried out by two organizations, the Bureau of Plant Industry and the Bureau of Forestry.

There are at least two distinguishing features in this multiple cross-classification. First, it permits a summation of various functions and programs served by

Table 5.1
Cross Classification of Government Budget by Function, Organization, Program and Project and Their Units of Work Measurement

Function	Organization	Programme	Project	Unit of work measurement
Agriculture	Bureau of Plant Industry	Increase in rice and corn production	1. Rice and corn research	Researches conducted
			2. Soil analysis	Soil samples analyzed
			3. Production and distribution of certified seeds	Cavans of seeds produced
			4. Control of rice and corn pests and deseases	Hectares controlled
			5. Demonstrations of improved farm practices and farmers' education	Demonstrations conducted
	Bureau of Forestry	Forest protection and management	1. Forest management and land uses	Number of hectares managed and leased
			2. Reforastation and afforestation	Number of hectares planted
			3. Domain use classification	Number of hectares classified
			4. Research	Number of research projects conducted
			5. Prevention of forest destruction	Number of hectares protected
			6. Scaling and lumber grading	Number of cubic metres of logs and lumber scaled and graded
			7. General administration	General administrative employment ratio and expense per man-year
Education	Bureau of Public Schools	Vacational education	1. Trade and industrial education	Students enrolled
			2. Agricultural education	Students enrolled
			3. Fishery education	Students enrolled
			4. Philippine nautical school	Students enrolled
			5. Training in home industries	Trainees enrolled
	Bureau of Public Libraries	Library and archives administration	1. Library extension service	Patrons served
			2. National library service	(a) No. of books, etc. catalogued, classified and processed
				(b) Patrons served
				(c) Indexing entries
			3. General administration	General administrative employment ratio and expense per man-year
General Government	Bureau of Internal Revenue	Administration and enforcement of internal revenue laws, special tax laws and regulations	1. Tax rulings and other legal services	Rulings issued
			2. Tax assessment	(a) Tax returns processed and/or assessed
				(b) Tax cases processed and/or
				(c) Tax investigations conducted
			3. Tax collection	Cases closed
			4. General administration	General administrative employment ratio; general administrative expense per man-year.
Health	Field Operations	Field health services	1. Rural health units	Units operated
			2. Dental services	Patients attended
			3. Social hygiene service	Number of cases handled
			4. Malaria eradication services	(a) Persons protected
				(b) Research activities
			5. Tuberculosis control services	Persons attended
			6. Environmental sanitation	Inspections conducted

Table 5.1 (Continued)
Cross Classification of Government Budget by Function, Organization, Program and Project and their Units of Work Measurement

Function	Organization	Programme	Project	Unit of work measurement
Health (continued)	Field operations (continued)	Hospital services	1. Operation of general hospitals	Number of free beds
			2. Operation of special hospitals	Patient days (a) Maternity (b) Children (c) Mental (d) Orthopedic (e) Communicable Diseases
			3. School of nursing	Persons trained
			4. School of midwifery	Persons trained
			5. Aid to puericulture	Narrative statement of purpose of aid
			6. Laundry plant	Number processed
	Bureau of Laboratories and Research	Laboratory examination production and research	1. General management	Administrative employment ratio and expense per man-year
			2. Pathological and macrobiological examination	Number of examinations performed
			3. Laboratory research	Number or research studies conducted
			4. Blood plasma dehydration	Cubic centimetres of blood products
			5. Sanitary chemical analysis	Number of examinations performed
			6. Vaccine production	Cubic centimetres manufactured
			7. Food and drug analysis	Number of examinations performed
Public works[a]	Bureau of Highways	Maintenance and repair service	1. National roads and bridges	(a) Kilometres of national roads serviced (b) Lineal metres of national bridges serviced
			2. Provincial roads and bridges	(a) Kilometres of provincial roads serviced (b) Lineal metres of provincial bridges serviced
			3. Municipal roads and bridges	Narrative statement of the project
			4. Toll roads	Toll roads serviced
	Bureau of Public Works	Construction (capital outlays)	1. Irrigation	Irrigable hectares serviced
			2. Buildings	Number of buildings
			3. River control and drainage	Number of projects
			4. Port facilities	Number of projects

Public Works here is not a function. It refers to the Department of Public Works and Communication whose expenditures fall under several functions as can be seen from the projects under the Programme of Construction in the Table. This however does not affect the purpose which is to illustrate the unit of work selected for projects.

Source: United Nations, *A Manual for Programe and Performance Budgeting.* United Nations publication Sales No. E.66.XVI.1 (1963), pp.64-65.

each organization for delegating their responsibilities. Second, it helps in the development and presentation of budget proposals with respect to the resource requirements and the measurement of accomplishments by each program.

In the United States, some agencies, notably the Department of Defense, which invented the PPBS program, still use the program, although the system was tried and abandoned in many civilian agencies of the federal government; some state governments in the United States also do. PPBS permits more realistic multiyear financial planning, which is particularly relevant to the strategic and long-term needs of national defense. The demise of PPBS in civil federal agencies of the United States and in other countries is due in part to the fact that a considerable amount of the budget is "uncontrollable." However, government administrations have benefited from the PPBS way of thinking and from the large-scale practice of quantitative analysis. They have become routine administrative methods for financial management decision making in the case of large projects.

D.2 Budget and Accounts on the Same Basis

In view of the close relationship between development planning and budgeting portrayed, government accounting is no longer limited to its traditional roles of satisfying the need for legislative accountability and providing for the administrative control of funds. Accounting is being increasingly recognized as a service to management, a service that provides data and information for planning, budgeting, monitoring, cost control, and performance evaluation.

The budget structure in traditional practice, with its organization-cum-object classification, has some merits but does not provide objective-oriented information on the execution and management of government activities; nor does it shed any light on the impact of government transactions on the rest of the economy. Similarly, conventional government accounting based on this structure is appropriate for legislative accountability but has severe limitations in terms of generating information for budget control and evaluation.

As illustrated previously, a program approach to budgeting, together with the adoption of suitable accounting procedures, is a promising way to remedy the defects mentioned. They place emphasis on programs to be achieved rather than categories of expenditure or organization. Such an approach can also provide data on the impact of government transactions on the rest of the economy and identify sources of funds, thus lending support to economic policy formulation.

Consistency in the classification and structure of government transactions in terms of economic and functional classification assumes significance in the harmonization of budget and accounts. Such consistency would facilitate the measurement of results of government activities from the available accounting information.

D.3 Accrual Accounting

Basically, an accrual budget is expressed in terms of costs to be incurred during a specific period rather than in terms of funds to be obligated or spent (based on an obligation or a cash basis). Similarly, on an accrual basis, revenues are recorded at the time when the right to collect them is generated, regardless of the time of cash receipt.

On an accrual basis, several kinds of financial data are generated to provide the extra financial information needed to strengthen financial control and to assist government authorities in the process of decision making. This information includes the costs of operations, the status of fixed assets, liabilities, earnings, and revenues; the receipt and disbursement of cash; and the periodic disclosure of financial conditions[6].

It should be noted, however, that the adoption of accrual accounting need not be envisaged as a replacement for the cash and obligation bases that are currently employed. A cash basis continues to be essential in managing fiscal, debts, and credit policies.

D.4 Long-Term Financial Survey

Financial management geared to short-term operations is simply not feasible without periodic forward planning covering a period of several years ahead, including both revenue and expenditure forecasting. This is particularly important in most capital projects, which take much more than a year to complete, especially as expenditure on them is often much greater in later periods.

The forward estimates serve several purposes in financial management. They identify continuing financial burdens resulting from current policies, offer the possibility of giving long-term assurance to various key agencies that they will be able to develop a coherent program that will not be subject to sudden cancellation, and provide a strategic analysis of major issues that suggest policy directons.

Long-term financial surveys usually cover a period of three to five years. They are susceptible to changing and unpredictable conditions and can be valid only within broad limits. Considerable judgment, and even guesswork, is required to match the estimated expenditure with prospective resources. In this respect, perspective planning is generally used as a framework for redirection of policies and redesigning of strategies rather than as a series of guidelines for day-to-day operations.

D.5 Financial Information Systems

Financial management relies on facts. Lack of statistical information makes it impossible to achieve sound financial management. In some developing countries—Indonesia, Mexico, and Turkey, for instance—difficulties in government budgeting are compounded by the lack of comprehensive data on external debt, which has been growing rapidly. Similarly, review and control of budget implementation have been hampered by fragmentary information on expenditure incurred and cash availability, inadequate accounting, and untimely submission of accounts. Even today, government accounts in many countries are published long after the close of the financial year, thus making them of little use for monitoring and evaluation purposes.

The financial information system (FIS) plays an important role in bridging the coordination gap between agencies. A comprehensive and integrated FIS should be governmentwide in scope, serving the needs of both the legislative and executive branches, by ensuring that consistent data are available across every agency network. Routine and special reports must be timely, useful, and understandable, and the reliability of the information must be assured.

The use of computers has significantly fostered the trend toward systematic organization and formalization of information. A computerized FIS handles a great volume of work efficiently and provides a simple conversational means for retrieving a variety of information through an interactive system. For instance, with the installation of electronic data processing (EDP) systems, monthly cashflow figures showing the amount spent and the balance can be obtained within a short time, and a comparison can be made between the spending profile and budget estimate for each block of expenditure in every agency. This is of crucial importance to cash management.

The computerization of FIS in many developing countries has yielded mixed results[7]. Countries such as India, Korea, Bahrain, Saudi Arabia, and Kenya have successfully implemented FIS and have found it a valuable instrument in financial management. Others, such as Guyana, Liberia, Papua New Guinea, and Tanzania, have experienced considerable problems after introducing EDP systems. In part, this is attributable to the lack of rationalization of the accounting systems and procedures to match the requirements of the EDP systems, and to a shortage of skilled and experienced staff. This suggests that as FIS becomes part of institutional arrangements, successful computerization must take into account the environmental situation and the social, cultural, and political forces at work in each country.

NOTES

1. This chapter is a revision of a paper prepared by Wuu-Long Lin that was presented at a meeting sponsored by the United Nations Department of Technical Co-Operation for Development, Interregional Training Program on Improving Government Accounting and Financial Reporting in Developing Countries, Banjul, Gambia, 13-24 April 1987.

2. This section draws heavily on the following materials: A. R. Prest, *Public Finance in Developing Countries,* 3rd edition (New York: St. Martin's Press, 1985), chapter 7, "Legislative and Administrative Aspects," United Nations, *Planning and Control of Public Current Expenditure—Lessons of Country Experience,* United Nations publication Sales

No. E.87.II.H.3 (1987), part B. chapter 3, "Means and Techniques of Controlling Public Current Expenditures"; United States General Accounting Office, *Managing the Cost of Government, Building an Effective Financial Management Structure,* GAO/Afmd-85-35-A (Washington, D.C., 1985), chapter 5, "Proposed Financial Process."

3. United States General Accounting Office, *Managing the Cost,* pp. 31-44.

4. This section relies heavily on United Nations, *Planning and Control,* pp. 49-69.

5. See United Nations, *Government Financial Management in Least Developed Countries,* United Nations publication Sales No. E.91.II.H.1 (1991).

6. United Nations, *Accrual Accounting in Developing Countries,* United Nations publication Sales No. E.84.II.H.2 (1984).

7. Ramgopal Agarwala, "Planning in Developing Countries, Lessons of Experience," World Bank Staff Working Papers No. 576 (Washington, D.C., 1989).

Chapter 6

CHANGING ROLES OF THE PUBLIC SECTOR IN FINANCIAL RESOURCE MOBILIZATION

A. INTRODUCTION

In early stages of development where financial resources for investment are limited, the public sector often plays an important role in the mobilization of financial resources.[1] The renewed concern over the mobilization of domestic financial resources is particularly keen at the present time in view of the rather dim prospects of obtaining capital flows from developed economies. In some cases there are net capital outflows from developing countries to developed countries. In addition, there has been increasing concern regarding the potential competition for external loans and aid among the independent states in the former Soviet Union, the Eastern European economies, and developing countries in other parts of the world.

This suggests that the prospects for growth in developing countries will continue to depend primarily on the domestic base instead of foreign capital. Therefore, the task of strengthening the role of the public sector in mobilizing domestic financial resources must be reexamined, especially at a time of increasing government deficits and heavy external debt burdens.

Table 6.1 sketches the sources of total investment. There are two sources of funds for a country's investment: foreign savings and domestic savings, which include public and private savings.

This chapter intends to provide an overview of recent trends and structural changes in domestic financial resources for development in the public sector in the context of a global perspective. It also highlights some relevant problems and changing policy issues in financial management of various countries. This discussion is particularly important in the monetized economies, where finance is the principal vehicle for orchestrating development and where the mobilization and management of domestic financial resources for accelerated growth are ma-

Table 6.1
Sources of Total Investment

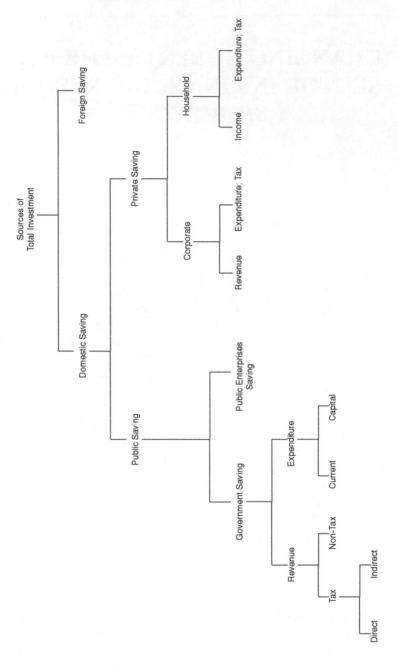

jor concerns. The discussion will focus primarily on developing economies but will also contrast the patterns of developing and developed economies.

B. MOBILIZATION OF GOVERNMENT REVENUE

Most developing countries have undertaken various reforms during the past decade to fight fiscal crisis. Reforms have resulted from the increased awareness of the needs to strengthen governmental capacities in raising revenues in order to revitalize economic and other development. However, there have been continuous debates regarding the optimal amount of additional revenue needed and the appropriate means of obtaining it. Tax revenues are a convenient source of needed funds, but to what extent should they be increased? High taxes may constitute a disincentive for saving and private investment and may also impose an undue burden on the poor.

B.1   Government Revenue in Relation to GDP

In general countries with high per capita income have a higher potential of raising revenue. As shown in Table 6.2, the relationship moves consistently, though not in a uniform pattern, with the country with lower per capita income having a lower ratio of government revenue to its GNP per capita. For instance, within the cluster with GNP per capita under US$300, such as Chad, Bangladesh, Nepal, and Uganda, the central government current revenue as a percentage of GNP in 1989 was under 10 percent. In contrast, within the cluster GNP per capita of more than $2,000, such as Malaysia, Oman, Singapore, and Kuwait, this ratio was more than 25 percent and above.

A few countries deviate from this pattern. Malawi and Ethiopia, for example, have incomes under US$300 GNP per capita, but their governments' current revenues as percentages of GNP frequently exceed 20 percent, which are substantially higher than those of most other countries with the same income level. In contrast, higher income countries such as Yugoslavia, Iran, and United Arab Emirates are classified in the category with GNP per capita of $2,000 and above, yet their government revenue as a ratio of GNP is only about 10 percent. These departures from the group pattern suggest that government revenue depends not only on the people's ability to pay in terms of their income but also on the government's ability to collect.

B.2   Revenue Trends

Government revenue tends to increase over time in order to match increases in public spending. Table 6.3 shows that central government current revenue as a

Table 6.2
Configuration of Countries According to Central Government Current Revenue as a Percentage of GNP and GNP per capita, 66 Developing Countries, 1989

GNP per capita, 1989 US Dollars	Countries in each GNP per capita group in which central government current revenue as percentage of GNP in 1989 was:				
	Under 10	10-14.9	15-19.9	20-24.9	25 and above
Under 300	Chad Bangladesh Nepal Sierra Leone Zaire Uganda		Nigeria Mali	Malawi	Ethiopia
300-449		Burkina Faso Central African Republic Ghana Zambia	India Pakistan	Kenya Sri Lanka	Togo
450-999	Guatemala	Philippines Bolivia	Liberia Indonesia Dominican Republic	Lesotho Papua New Guinea Mauritania Morocco Syrian Arab Republic	Zimbabwe Egypt Arab Republic
1000-1999	Peru El Salvador	Ecuador Columbia Paraguay	Cameron Turkey Thlaland	Mauritius Jordan	Botswana Chile Panama Tunisia Costa Rica Poland
2000 & over	Yugoslavia Iran United Arab Emirates	Argentina	Korea Rep. of Mexico	Uruguay Venezuela	Malaysia Nicaragua South Africa Brazil Hungary Oman Singapore Kuwait Trinidad and Tobago Portugal

Source: Tabulated from World Bank, *World Development Report 1991*, New York, Oxford University Press (1991), pp. 226–227.

Table 6.3
Trends of Central Government Total Current Revenue as a
Percentage of GNP by Major Income Group, 1972 vs. 1989

Income Group	GNP per Capita, US$ 1989a/	Central government total current revenue as a percentage of GNP a/		
		1972	1989	Increment between 1989 and 1972
1. Developing economies (51 countries)	1,772	16.0	18.9	2.9
Low-income	296	12.4	14.8	2.4
Lower-middle income	1,244	15.0	19.0	4.0
Upper-middle	3,531	23.6	23.4	-.2
High income	12,763	25.6	31.6	6.0
2. Developed Market economies (l9 countries)	17,588	28.3	35.4	7.1

Source: Computed from World Bank, *World Development Report 1991,* New York, Oxford University Press (1991), pp. 226–227.

a/ Computation based on an unweighted average.

percentage of GNP increased in all income groups of both developing economies and developed market economies from 1972 to 1989. Furthermore, it also shows that the increment of government revenues during this period is larger in the higher income group at 7.1 percentage points as compared to the 2.9 percentage points on the average for developing economies.

Generally speaking, the lower central government revenue and its slower growth path in low-income economies can largely be attributed to weak commodity prices and low rates or even stagnation of economic growth. Nevertheless, it is generally believed that the tax potential in many low-income countries has not been fully exploited. Another major cause of poor revenue performance in the lower-income countries is tax evasion due to ineffective tax administration.

B.3   Revenue Structure

Table 6.4 shows the contrasting patterns of tax and nontax revenue of countries in the major income categories in 1972 and 1989. There have been several observations made on revenue structure and its evolution over time:

(a)   On the basis of country grouping average, nontax revenue accounts for 21.9 percent of central government total current revenue. This ratio in a developing economy is about two times the ratio of a developed economy. This ratio increased slightly between 1972 and 1989. However, nontax revenue forms a dominant part of government revenue in a number of countries, for example, it accounted for more than 60 percent of total revenue in 1989 in Brazil, Oman, and Kuwait. In the case of oil exporting countries, profits and royalties from petroleum resources provide the bulk of nontax government revenue.

(b)   Tax revenue has consistently accounted for about 80 percent of government finances, although it experienced a minor decrease in terms of its ratio to government current revenue between 1972 and 1989.

(c)   There were no significant shifts in the structure of taxation away from indirect taxes toward direct taxes during the period 1972 to 1989, but the tax structure varies among country groups. Within the developing economies, the major sources of tax revenue are taxes on international trade and transactions in low-income economies, particularly in Sub-Saharan Africa. This contrasts the major sources of tax revenue resulting from taxes on domestic goods and services in lower-middle income economies, and from taxes on income, profit, and capital gains in upper-middle income economies. In countries such as Uganda and Lesotho, taxes on international trade and transactions accounted for more than 50 percent of total government current revenue in 1989. The dependence of taxes on international trade reflects the extent of the weakness of the developing countries.

Table 6.4
Central Government Current Revenue Structure by Major Income Group, 1972 and 1989

As a percentage of central government total current revenue a/

Income Group	GNP per capita US $ a/ 1989	Taxes on Income, Profit and Capital Gain 1972	Taxes on Income, Profit and Capital Gain 1989	Domestic Taxes on Goods and Services 1972	Domestic Taxes on Goods and Services 1989	Taxes on International Trade and Transactions 1972	Taxes on International Trade and Transactions 1989	Taxes on Security Contribution 1972	Taxes on Security Contribution 1989	Other Taxes b/ 1972	Other Taxes b/ 1989	Current Non-tax Revenue 1972	Current Non-tax Revenue 1989
1. Developing Economies (51 countries)		22.9	22.4	23.9	26.5	24.7	21.9	3.7	3.7	6.8	3.6	18.0	21.9
Low Income	296	25.5	23.1	24.4	27.2	32.2	31.3	0	0.4	3.9	3.1	14.0	14.9
Lower-middle Income	1,244	18.2	22.4	26.6	29.4	27.2	20.8	5.6	5.4	6.5	3.7	15.9	18.3
Upper-Middle Income	3,531	26.7	27.3	19.5	19.0	5.5	8.5	9.8	9.0	16.0	3.7	22.5	32.5
High Income	12,763	31.0	7.2	12.4	19.9	4.2	1.3	0.0	1.0	5.3	3.7	47.1	66.9
2. Developed Market Economies (19 countries)	17,588	35.7	35.9	28.3	26.9	4.3	1.6	19.6	22.7	3.5	3.4	7.6	9.5

Source: Computed from World Bank, *World Development Report 1991*, New York, Oxford University Press (1991), pp. 226–227.

a/ Computation based on an unweighted average
b/ Computed as residual

(d)   Taxes on social security contributions account for only a small propor-
       tion of tax revenue in developing economies. They are consistently higher
       in higher-income economies than in lower-income economies.

(e)   In comparison with the developing economies as a group, the developed
       market economies have a relatively higher proportion of tax than nontax
       revenue. They also have a higher proportion of direct taxes on income,
       profit and capital gains, and social security contributions, and a lower
       proportion of taxes on international trade and transactions.

B.4 Tax Reform

Because of extensive fiscal deficits and limited access to new borrowing, most
developing countries have little opportunity for deliberate reductions in taxation
in the future. However, in order to increase taxes and to assess their economic
impact, governments must recognize that the primary reason for taxation is to
raise the required revenue to promote socioeconomic development, thus improving the welfare of the people. Thus, any negative economic effects of taxation
must be balanced with the beneficial aspects of public expenditure programs.

Some potentially negative economic effects of taxation are disincentives to
work and to save caused by high taxes, poverty traps attibutable to broad-based
taxes on low-income families, and adverse effects on investment in physical and
human capital and on innovations. They also include adverse effects on export
promotion due to high taxes on international trade and transactions and pressures resulting from the interaction of inflation and taxation.[2]

Different measures of tax reform have been taken by many developing countries with varying degrees of success.[3]

For example, tax reforms have concentrated on expanding taxation bases in
order to avoid higher tax rates and adverse effects on incentives to work and to
save in such countries as Colombia, Indonesia, Jamaica, and Malawi. Some reforms have also tried to promote equity by limiting tax deductions for the wealthy
and by avoiding taxes on the poor. Some tax loopholes were closed in the 1989
tax reform in Guatemala.

Examples of such tax reforms are the elimination of the wholesale tax as a
means of stimulating investment incentives in the 1983 tax reform of Indonesia
and the introduction of a value-added tax with the objective of generating substantial revenue in such countries as Brazil, Korea, and Turkey.

Tax reform is a long-term task and requires periodic changes in order to accommodate external circumstances or internal needs, as was in the case of Colombia in a series of major tax reforms in 1953, 1960, and 1986.

C. PLANNING AND CONTROL OF PUBLIC EXPENDITURE

The last decade has been characterized by rapid growth and diversified public expenditure patterns. However, governments have also recognized the need for more rigorous control of public expenditure because of factors such as frequent recurrences of government overspending, mismanagement of public enterprises, and inefficient government administration. Different governments have taken different steps to trim public expenditure with the common goal of regulating its growth so that it will neither detrimentally affect the economy nor exceed the annual resources available.

C.1   Government Expenditure in Relation to GDP

Table 6.5 examines whether the relative importance of government expenditure in the economy is a function of the level of development. Each of the two variables, GNP per capita in 1989 and central government expenditure as a percentage of GNP, is classified into five strata, thus creating a total of 25 cells.

In terms of the 1989 data for 56 developing countries, no clear patterns surfaced between these two variables. A great majority of developing countries are in the lower-middle stratum of central government expenditure of 15 to 24.9 percent of GNP. These countries are spread unevenly over various income strata, ranging from the lowest stratum of GNP per capita under U.S.$300 to the highest stratum of $2,000 and over. Similarly, in the highest stratum, with central government expenditure of 35 to 39.9 percent of GNP, for instance, GNP per capita in countries such as Ethiopia and Malawi is as low as under US$300, whereas countries like South Africa and Trinidad and Tobago have GNP per capita as high as US$2,000 and above.

These findings suggest that the relative importance of the public sector in the economy measured by the ratio of central government expenditure to GNP has determinants other than GNP per capita.

C.2   Size and Growth of Aggregate Public Expenditure

During the 1960s and 1970s, the growth of government revenue in many countries coincided with a trend of rising recurrent expenditure, particularly because of indiscriminant hiring of staff. However, in the 1980s countries were forced by financial constraints to regulate the accelerating rate of growth in public spending.

It appears from Table 6.6 that central government expenditure as a percentage of GNP has been consistently higher in the industrialized countries than in the developing countries. The increment of this ratio over time is larger in the former than in the latter. This ratio increased by 8.7 percentage points (from 28.6 per-

Table 6.5

Configuration of Countries According to Central Government Expenditure as Percentage of GNP and GNP per capita, 56 Developing Countries, 1989

GNP per capita 1989 US Dollars	Countries in each GNP per capita group in which central government expenditure as a percentage of GNP in 1989 was:				
	Under 15	**15-24.9**	**25-34.9**	**35-39.9**	**40 and above**
Under 300		Nepal Zaire	Nigeria Mali	Ethiopia Malawi	
300-449	Burkina Faso Ghana	India Pakistan Zambia	Kenya Central African Republic Sri Lanka Togo		

450-999	Philippines
	Guatemala
		Indonesia
		Liberia
		Bolivia
		Dominican
		  Republic
			Mauritania
			Morocco
			Papua New
			  Guinea
			Syrian Arab
			  Republic
					Zimbabwe
					Egypt, Arab
					  Republic
					Bhutan

1000-1999	Colombia Peru Paraguay El Salvador	Ecuador Turkey Mauritius Cameroon Thailand	Chile Costa Rica Panama	Jordan	Botswana Tunisia Poland

2000 and over	Yugoslavia	Singapore
		Korea, Rep.of
		Iran, Islamic
		  Republic
		United Arab
		  Emirates
			Brazil
			Uruguay
			Kuwait
				South Africa
				Trinidad and
				  Tobago
					Hungary
					Portugal
					Oman

Source: Tabulated from World Bank, *World Development Report 1991,* New York, Oxford University Press (1991), pp. 224–225.

Table 6.6

Trends of Central Government Total Expenditures as a Percentage of GNP by Major Income Group, 1972 vs. 1989

		Central government expenditure as a percentage of GNP a/		
Income Group	GNP per Capita, US$ 1989a/	1972	1989	Increment between 1989 and 1972
1. Developing economies (42 countries)	1,772	20.7	23.1	2.4
Low-income	296	16.7	22.9	6.2
Lower-middle income	1,244	20.2	22.6	2.4
Upper-middle income	3,531	29.7	25.4	-4.3
High income	12,763	18.3	22.4	4.1
2. Developed Market Economies (I8 countries)	17,588	28.6	37.3	8.7

Source: Computed from World Bank, *World Development Report 1991,* New York, Oxford University Press (1991), pp. 224–225.

a/ Computation based on an unweighted average.

cent in 1972 to 37.3 percent in 1989) in the developed market economies but increased by only 2.4 percentange points (from 20.7 percent in 1972 to 23.1 percent in 1989) in the developing countries. Within the developing economies, both low-income and lower-middle income economies slightly increased their central government expenditure as a percentage of GNP, by 6.2 and 2.4 percentage points between 1972 and 1989, respectively. There was a slight decrease of government spending relative to GNP in the upper-middle income group of developing economies. This is largely the result of a rapid decrease of government spending in some oil exporting countries due to a shortfall of oil revenue. For instance, between 1972 and 1989 this ratio decreased 14 percentage points in Oman and 12 percentage points in Iran.

The group average of government spending as a percentage of GNP as reported in Table 6.6 conceals a wide range of variations among countries. Although there is no specific formula for determining an appropriate size or share of government spending, country comparisons show a wide range of average public spending within the same income group. For instance, central government expenditure as a ratio of GNP in 1989 was as high as 45 percent in Bhutan, 50 percent in Botswana, 59 percent in Hungary, and 58 percent in Ireland. In all these cases, the ratio was substantially higher than that of other countries in the same income group. On the other hand, some countries have substantially a lower level of public spending in comparison with that of other countries in the same income group. For instance, central government expenditure as a ratio of GNP in 1989 was as low as 11 percent in Burkina Faso, 12 percent in Peru, 5 percent in Yugoslavia, and 17 percent in Japan. In all these cases, the ratio was substantially lower than that of other countries in the same group.

In most developing countries, the sharp reduction of the already low public spending during the structural adjustment period resulted in shortages of school textbooks and medicines, as well as negligence in the maintenance of infrastructure. As evidenced in Costa Rica, economic and social infrastructure has been negatively affected by budgetary cuts.

The need for maintaining some key programs such as social and infrastructural services does not necessarily imply an increase in public expenditure. Much can be done through better targeting and allocation of expenditures, strengthening of public sector management, and enhancement of the involvement of local communities.

C.3   Composition of Public Expenditure

Policymakers often faced major challenges on expenditure allocation during the austere period of structural adjustment, attempting to accommodate both ideology and practical considerations. A few large programs frequently constitute a major portion of central government expenditures. For examples, in 1989 in Bhutan, 51 percent of public expenditure was directed toward economic services;

in Uruguay and Sweden more than 50 percent was directed toward housing, amenities, social security, and welfare; and in Syrian Arab Republic, United Arab Emirates, and Oman more than 40 percent was spent on national defense. The functional categories of central government expenditure classified by major income group in 1972 and 1989 are presented in Table 6.7.[4] The following are the major findings:

(a) The greatest distinction in central government expenditure between developed and developing countries is the weight of housing, amenities, social security, and welfare, which accounted for as much as 38.4 percent of total outlay in developed economies in 1989. This represents more than three times that in the developing countries. Expenditures on economic services were 10.1 percent of total outlay in the developed market economies in 1989: slightly more than one half of that in developing countries.

(b) In both developing and developed economies, structural adjustments did not bring drastic changes in the functional structure of central government outlays between 1972 and 1989. The most obvious change is the weight of economic services, which decreased by 6.1 percentage points from 1972 to 19.6 percent in 1989 in the developing countries, and by 4.6 percentage points from 1972 to 10.1 percent in 1989 in the developed market economies. As has been observed in Costa Rica, Guatemala, and many other countries, such cuts had adverse effects on maintenance and rehabilitation of economic infrastructure.

(c) The weight of other general administration expenditure not included increased by 5.3 percentage points from 1972 to 33.3 percent in 1989 in the developing economies and by 7.6 percentage points to 25.5 percent in the developed market economies. Attempts have been made by most countries to restrict expenditures on salaries, wages, and general administration through careful reviews of personnel and job requirements, elimination of overlap and duplication of functions among various agencies, and decentralization to local agencies.

(d) In all developed market economies, the share of national defense in total outlay was progressively reduced. The average decreased from 12.3 percent in 1972 to 8.8 percent in 1989. Among the developing countries, a mixture of increases and decreases in defense expenditures as a share of total outlay is obsered during the two periods. On the average, the share remained quite stable, registering a slight decrease from 14.7 percent in 1972 to 14.2 percent in 1989. Some countries had a considerable reduction, such as Nigeria, with a substantial decrease of 37.4 percentage points from 1972 to 2.8 percent in 1989. However, other countries, such as Kuwait and United Arab Emirates, experienced an increase of 11.5 and 19.5 percentage points during the two periods, respectively.

Table 6.7
Central Government Expenditure Structure by Major Income Group, 1972 and 1989

As a percentage of Central Government Expenditure a/

Income Group	Defense		Education		Health		Housing; Amenities Social Security and Welfare		Economic Services		Other b/	
	1972	1989	1972	1989	1972	1989	1972	1989	1972	1989	1972	1989
1. Developing Economies (36 countries)	14.7	14.2	14.7	14.1	5.4	6.3	11.5	12.5	25.7	19.6	28.0	33.3
Low Income	13.9	9.2	13.5	11.6	5.1	5.0	4.7	5.4	25.1	24.3	37.7	44.5
Lower-middle Income	12.3	14.4	17.9	17.0	6.4	7.8	14.3	13.7	26.8	18.0	22.3	29.1
Upper Middle Income	18.1	16.7	8.4	10.9	3.3	5.0	19.8	23.4	29.3	18.4	21.1	25.6
High Income	22.7	28.3	15.7	16.0	5.9	6.5	8.1	12.6	14.9	11.6	32.7	25.0
2. Developed Market Economies (16 countries)	12.3	8.8	10.0	7.8	8.9	9.4	36.2	38.4	14.7	10.1	17.9	25.5

Source: Computed from World Bank, *World Development Report 1991*, New York, Oxford University Press (1991), pp. 224–225.

a/ Computation based on an unweighted average.
b/ Other covers expenditure for the general administration of government not included elsewhere; for a few economies it also includes amount that could not be allocated to other components.

Different measures and techniques have been adopted by various countries for the management and control of public expenditure in order to accommodate different economic and administrative settings. This subject will be further discussed in Chapter 7.

D. THE GOVERNMENT AS SAVER

The difference between government current revenue and current expenditure is government savings. A government is described as dissaving when its current revenue falls short of its current expenditure. Some governments have placed emphasis on government savings. Many governments exert budget-cutting strategies through various fiscal means, partly because of the increasing burden of interest payments on public bonds issued for financing budget deficits. However, it is not easy to raise the government savings beyond a certain level. While confronting the constraints in raising tax revenue, government recurrent development expenditures on such services as education and health tend to increase in the development process. They often become as significant as investment in physical assets.

D.1   Trend of Domestic Savings

Countries with low economic growth tend to face more serious constraints in mobilizing domestic financial resources for promoting economic development. This is a manifestation of a vicious cycle in a depressed economy. It appears from Table 6.8 that the low-income countries as a group, excluding China and India, have the lowest gross domestic savings as a ratio to GDP, at 12.3 percent in 1989. By geographical region (see Table 6.9), the Sub-Saharan Africa region, with a ratio of 13 percent in 1987, is the lowest in the low- and middle-income group. The ratio in Sub-Saharan Africa is even lower than that in highly indebted countries, where this ratio is 21 percent.

Domestic savings consist of public and private savings. It is observed consistently, although not with the same magnitude, that public savings are negative in every low- and middle-income group (see Table 6.8). Consequently, private savings are the only domestic financial resources for promoting economic development. Specifically, it is the household sector's surplus that finances the deficits of the government and corporate sectors. In this regard, the government should play an important role in encouraging household savings. This can be done through creating easier access to financial institutions and better financial intermediation. Therefore, it is a pressing need to strengthen and to reestablish an operational framework for the existing banking system, which in some countries is in danger of breaking down. This requires some special government measures to promote more efficient capital and money markets. Meanwhile, the less formal

Table 6.8
Gross Domestic Savings by Major Income Groups, 1989

Income group	As a percentage of GDP (weighted average), 1989		
	Gross Domestic Savings	Public Savings[a]	Private Savings[b]
(1)	(2)	(3)	(4)
Developing economies			
Low income	14.1	—	—
— China and India	28.5	—	—
— Other low income	12.3	-4.3	16.6
Middle income	21.4	-16.0	37.4
—Low middle income	18.8	-19.8	38.6
—Upper middle income	29.1	-4.8	33.9
High-income	41.5	3.2	38.3
Developed market economies	23.8	2.2	21.6

Source: Tabulated from World Bank, *World Development Report 1991,* New York, Oxford University Press (1991), pp. 220–221, 224–225.

a/ Current account budget surplus or deficit.

b/ Residual of gross domestic savings and public savings.

Table 6.9
Gross Domestic Savings by Regions, Low and Middle Income Economies, 1987

	GNP per capita (Weighted Average) 1987 US Dollars	As a percentage of GDP 1987, (weighted average)		
		Gross domestic savings[a]	Public savings[b]	Private savings
Low-and middle-income	700	25	-7.7	32.7
By region				
Sub-Saharan Africa	330	13	—	
East Asia	470	35	—	
South Asia	290	19	-8.5	27.5
Europe, Middle East & North Africa	1,940	—	-7.2	
Latin America and Caribbean	1,790	20	-10.2	30.2
Highly indebted countries	1,430	21	-9.2	30.2

[a] Current account budget surplus or deficit.

[b] Residual of gross domestic savings and public savings.

Source: World Bank, *World Development Report 1989,* New York, Oxford University Press (1989), pp. 180–181, 184–185.

savings and loan associations in remote areas should be promoted to link with the formal financial institutions. This linkage of the savings and loan associations and the banking system is important because in the remote areas and in the low income households, financial activities will be carried out more efficiently by those less formal savings and loan associations.

Within the developing economies, average private saving tends to become higher as income increases. As observed in Table 6.8, the low middle-income group has the highest private savings as a ratio to gross domestic savings at 38.6 percent in 1989. In contrast, this ratio is 16.6 percent in other low-income economies, excluding China and India.

As observed in Table 6.10, during 1965 and 1989, there was a slight decrease of gross domestic savings as a ratio to GDP on the average in the developing economies. This is in contrast with an increment of savings in other income groups of the developing economies during the two periods observed. Other low-income group countries, excluding China and India, registered a 9 percentage point decrease. However, some individual countries that were not reported in the group average of Table 6.10 registered negative savings in 1989 with a decrease of 25 percentage points or more from 1965, for example, Zambia, Lesotho, Saudi Arabia, and Kuwait.

D.2   Decreased Government Savings

As shown in Table 6.11, 43 of 53 developing countries showed government dissavings in 1989. These statistics give cause for much concern in the case of countries such as Brazil, Nepal, Madagascar, and Zimbabwe, where the government deficit as a percentage of GNP was -8.0 percent or higher. Table 6.11 also indicates that government deficit as a ratio of GDP is higher in the majority of lower-income economies. Moreover, every regional average of developing countries indicates that there was a government deficit every year from 1981 to 1989 (see Table 6.12). It also shows that the central government fiscal deficit as a percentage of GDP increased from an average of 2.6 percent in 1981 to 11.8 percent in 1989 in the Middle East, and from 5.7 percent in 1981 to 6.5 percent in 1989 in Africa.

The increasing burden of government deficits illustrates that as economic development proceeds, the contribution of government savings has been deteriorating. The phenomenon of decreased government savings can be best explained with reference to a study by Please.[5] The study states that while government has been successful in increasing the ratio of tax revenue to GDP, the proportion of public savings has tended to decline as a result of a more rapid increase in government current expenditures. In other words, there is a ratchet effect of an increase in public consumption that is induced by an increase in taxation.

Table 6.10
Change of Gross Domestic Savings by Major Income Groups,
1965 and 1989

Income Group	Gross Domestic Savings as a Percentage of GDP, %		
	1965	1989	Percentage point change between 1965 and 1989.
Developing economies			
(77 countries)	17	16	- 1
Low-income	16	8	- 8
— China and India	20	29	+ 9
— Other low-income	16	7	- 9
Middle income	17	21	+ 4
— Lower-middle income	15	19	+ 4
— Upper-middle income	23	28	+ 5
High-income economies	29	33	+ 4
Developed market economies (21 countries)	22	24	+ 2

Source: Tabulated from World Bank, *World Development Report 1991*, New York, Oxford University Press (1991), pp. 220–221.

Table 6.11
Configuration of Countries According to Overall Surplus/Deficit as a Percentage of GNP, 53 Countries, 1989

Countries in each GNP per capita group in which overall surplus/deficit as a percentage of GNP in 1989 was

GNP per capita 1989 US Dollars	Surplus	Deficit			
		-0.1 to -3.99%	-4.0 to -7.9%	-8.0 to -II.9%	-12.0% and above
Under 300			Ethiopia Malawi Zair Mali	Nepal Madagascar	
300-449	Ghana Burkina Faso	Togo	Kenya India Pakistan Zambia Sri Lanka		

450-999	Bhutan	Indonesia
		Philippines
		Papua New
		  Guinea
		Mauritania
		Bolivia
		Guatemala
		Syrian, Arab
		Rep.
			Liberia
			Morocco
			Egypt, Arab
			  Rep.
				Zimbabwe	

1000-1999	Ecuador Botswana Paraguay Thailand	Colombia Cameroon El Salvador Chile Costa Rica Poland Mauritius	Peru Turkey Tunisia Panama	Jordan	

2000 & over	Korea, Rep.of
	Yugoslavia
	Singapore
		Uruguay
		Hungary
		Iran, Islamic
		  Rep. of
		United Arab
		  Emirates
			South Africa
			Trinidad and
			  Tobago
			Portugal
				Oman	Brazil

Source: Tabulated from World Bank, *World Development Report 1991*, New York, Oxford University Press, pp. 224–225.

Table 6.12
Central Government Fiscal Balance as a Percentage of GDP,
Developing Countries, 1981–1989

Region	Central government fiscal balance as a percentage of GDP								
	1981	1982	1983	1984	1985	1986	1987	1988	1989
Developing countries	-3.8	-5.3	-5.3	-4.6	-4.2	-6.0	-6.0	-5.8	-4.8
By region									
Africa	-5.7	-6.8	-7.6	-5.1	-4.8	-6.1	-7.9	-8.0	-6.5
Asia	-3.1	-4.2	-3.3	-2.7	-3.0	-4.1	-3.6	-3.7	-3.9
Europe	-4.7	-2.5	-2.4	-2.6	-2.7	-2.1	-2.I	-2.2	-2.7
Middle East	-2.6	-6.8	-10.0	-10.2	-8.2	-13.9	-12.5	-13.0	-11.8
Western Hemisphere	-4.1	-6.2	-4.8	-3.8	-3.3	-4.7	-5.6	-4.8	-2.2

Source: Tabulated from International Monetary Fund, *World Economic Survey* (Washington, D.C., April 1988), p.144.

D.3 Cutting Budget Deficits

Government budgetary deficits continue to pose a major problem for economic policy in most developing countries, in spite of the many structural adjustments made to contain these deficits.[6] Very often the increase in the budget deficit is used to finance the interest payment on the existing deficit. This extra burden of higher public borrowing may create undesirable impacts on economic performance, known as the crowding-out effect: a reduction in private activities, such as private consumption and investment, resulting from a rise in public borrowing and expenditures. A rise in public expenditure typically leads to budget deficits that will subsequently be financed through public high-yield-bond issues. This financing may cause inflation, high interest rates, disincentives to private investment, and increased unemployment.[7] Although it is difficult to generalize about the validity of this contention, it is generally believed that continuing rapid growth of government expenditure, if unchecked, would cause economic problems.

Most developing countries in Asia have pursued rather cautious public finance policies and have achieved significant improvements in fiscal balance in recent years.[8] India adopted flexible expenditure and revenue policies in 1987 to prevent a sharp deterioration of the fiscal position during a severe drought. In China, the government delayed its price liberalization and tightened its credit controls as the primary measures in preventing further acceleration of inflation.

Similarly, in the Western Hemisphere, developing countries such as Argentina, Brazil, and Mexico have improved their fiscal balances in recent years through the adoption of stabilization programs. A few highly indebted countries in that region, notably Chile and Colombia, have pursued more prudent financial policies and have managed to contain inflation. Some African countries, such as Ghana, Senegal, and Tanzania, have undertaken fiscal reforms to broaden revenuc bases and to reduce expenditures, thereby achieving significant improvements in their fiscal positions in recent years.

Nonetheless, highly indebted countries like Côte d'Ivoire, Nigeria, and many Sub-Saharan African nations, have continued to experience a sharp deterioration in their fiscal balance. This situation is attributed to factors such as declining prices of oil and export commodities, poor production, narrow tax revenue base, and relatively ineffective fiscal policies. Similarly, fiscal balances in the Middle Eastern countries were weakened considerably by the sharp decline in oil revenues in the latter part of the 1980s.

E. INTERNATIONAL FINANCING AND EXTERNAL DEBT

In conjunction with government deficits, many developing countries have incurred mounting debt-servicing problems since the 1982 debt crisis. Although the danger of widespread defaults has been greatly reduced, the adverse impact of the heavy debt-servicing burden has hindered restoration of economic growth.

This suggests that the debt strategy pursued since 1982 needs to be revised to serve the interests of both creditors and debtors more effectively.

E.1 External Debt in Relation to GDP

The configuration of countries presented in Table 6.13 examines 1987 data of 79 developing countries to determine whether a countrys's debt-servicing capacity in terms of external public debt service as a percentage of GNP is associated with its level of development in terms of GNP per capita. On the basis of the pattern in terms of numbers of countries in each group, it is observed that countries with higher GNP per capita tend to have higher potential for external financing.

A number of individual countries deviate from this pattern. For instance, Mauritania is in the low-income stratum of US$300 to US$449 GNP per capita but is also in the highest category of external public debt services of 8 percent and above of GNP. Peru and the Arab Republic of Syria are in the higher middle-income stratum of US$1,000 to US$1,999 GNP per capita, but are in the lowest category of external public debt service, under 2 percent of GNP. This suggests that many factors other than income influence a country's ability to secure external financing.

E.2 Trend of the External Debt Situation

Beginning in 1979, a growing number of countries began to experience difficulties in meeting their debt payment obligations. The debt crisis became a headline in 1982 when Mexico suffered from a sharp decline in export earnings due to weakened oil prices and announced a de facto moratorium on amortization payments to commercial creditors.

It appears from Table 6.14 that external debt as a percentage of GDP increased steadily for developing countries as a group, from 27.8 percent in 1981 to a peak of 38.1 percent in 1986. It then gradually declined to 32.3 percent in 1990.[9, 10] A similar pattern is also found when external debt or debt service is expressed as a ratio of exports of goods and services. These external debt and debt service ratios declined in recent years but remained high. Additional sources of financing have been regarded as critical elements in dealing with debt-servicing problems and restoring economic growth but have not been forthcoming on a significant scale.

By geographic region, the ratios mentioned are highest in Africa and in the Western Hemisphere and are lowest in Asia. For instance, debt service as a percentage of exports of goods and services in 1990 was 26.8 percent in Africa and 43.0 percent in the Western Hemisphere, compared with only 9.4 percent in Asia. Most low-income countries, particularly in Africa, were severely affected by the downturn in world trade and the weakened export commodity prices. Nonethe-

Table 6.13
Configuration of Countries According to External Public Debt Service as a Percentage of GNP, 79 Developing Countries, 1987

GNP per capita, 1987 US Dollars	Countries in each GNP per capita group in which external public debt service as a percentage of GNP in 1987 was				
	Under 2%	2-3.9%	4-5.9%	6-7.9%	8% and above
Under 300	Bhutan Chad Bangladesh Nepal LAO PDR Burkina Faso Mali Uganda China Somalia	Ethiopia Tanzania Burundi	Zaire Niger Togo	Malawi Madagascar Zambia	
300-449	India Rwanda Sierra Leone Sudan Haiti	Benin Central African Rep. Lesotho Nigeria Ghana	Sri Lanka	Kenya Yemen, PDR	Mauritania

450-999	Liberia
	Nicaragua
		Bolivia
		Yemen Arab
		  Rep.
		Dominican Rep.
		El Salvador
		Cameroon
			Egypt, Arab
			  Republic
			Thailand
			Guatemala
			Ecuador
				Senegal
				Zimbabwe
				Philippines
				Morocco
				Papua New
				  Guinea
				Cote d' Ivoire
				Honduras
					Indonesia
					Congo, People's
					  Rep.
					Jamaica

1000-1999	Peru Syrian, Arab Rep.		Ecuador Botswana Mauritius Costa Rica	Turkey Columbia Chile Mexico	Tunisia Jordan Malaysia
2000 & over		Brazil Gabon Singapore	Uruguay Argentina Venezuela	Panama Algeria	Korea, Rep. of Trinidad and Tobago Oman

Source: Tabulated from World Bank, *World Development Report 1991*, New York, Oxford University Press (1991), pp. 210–211.

Table 6.14
Total External Debt and Debt Services, Developing Countries,
1981–1990

	1981	1982	1983	1984	1985	1986	1987	1988	1989	1990
1. External debt as a percentage of GDP, %										
Developing countries	27.8	31.0	32.8	34.1	36.0	38.1	37.7	35.6	33.7	32.3
By region										
Africa	31.4	35.4	38.2	41.9	46.9	49.8	48.6	49.8	50.5	49.9
Asia	18.6	21.4	22.5	23.4	26.1	28.8	27.6	25.1	22.5	21.3
Europe	34.2	34.7	37.1	40.6	44.5	42.9	45.1	42.3	39.1	37.1
Middle East	19.2	22.5	24.4	25.8	27.3	31.2	31.0	30.8	31.0	30.2
Western Hemisphere	39.8	43.7	46.8	46.5	45.4	45.5	46.0	44.0	42.8	41.1
2. External debt as a percentage of exports of goods and services, %										
Developing countries	95.8	120.0	134.8	134.3	150.8	170.8	158.7	141.9	132.1	126.6
By region										
Africa	119.3	154.5	170.6	170.5	191.3	244.9	249.2	248.9	241.9	243.9
Asia	73.8	87.1	92.5	88.3	101.8	103.0	89.1	76.1	69.6	65.7
Europe	136.9	145.0	149.1	145.4	160.5	168.4	169.0	146.2	133.9	127.0
Middle East	34.6	47.6	63.6	72.0	84.9	116.3	109.8	116.8	112.3	110.7
Western Hemisphere	209.8	271.8	292.5	274.6	296.9	353.0	346.3	305.0	297.3	289.8
3. Debt service as a percentage of exports of goods and services, %										
Developing countries	16.2	19.7	18.6	20.0	21.3	23.0	20.3	19.6	18.9	17.5
By region										
Africa	17.0	21.2	22.9	26.6	29.1	29.1	25.4	28.8	29.0	26.8
Asia	9.9	12.3	11.9	12.3	14.4	14.5	14.8	11.4	10.6	9.4
Europe	21.8	22.9	20.7	21.7	23.7	26.5	25.9	25.3	23.8	21.4
Middle East	5.0	6.5	8.3	10.0	10.3	14.0	12.6	12.8	12.6	12.3
Western Hemisphere	43.9	54.0	43.3	42.7	42.1	47.2	37.0	41.6	43.2	43.0

Source: Tabulated from International Monetary Fund, *World Economic Survey,* (Washington D.C.,
April 1988), pp. 192–194.

less, there is an optimistic expectation that the debt situation will improve and stabilize as a result of policy changes for structural adjustment and export growth adopted by most countries.

E.3 Debt Reduction Strategies

International debt reduction strategy has evolved in recent years.[11] The so-called market menu approach has become an important element in the evolving debt strategy as far as debt owed to commercial banks is concerned. This approach was also supported by the international financial community including the International Monetary Fund in 1987. According to this market menu approach, the major debt reduction options to date have involved debt buy-backs and exchanges of existing debt for new instruments that include collateral and swaps of domestic equity for foreign debt. Buy-backs have been used by Bolivia, Chile, and Mexico: debt-equity conversions have been used by Chile, Brazil, and Mexico.

As for official bilateral creditors, a major step was taken on 21 June 1988 at the Toronto Summit of the seven major industrial countries (the Group of Seven). As a follow-up of this initiative, in the fall of 1988, the Paris Club of official creditors agreed on the following new options[12]:

(a)   *Partial write-off:* One third of the debt services originally due during the period being renegotiated would be forgiven. The remainder would be rescheduled under fairly standard terms for low-income countries with a 14-year maturity with 8-year grace period at market interest rates;

(b)   *Extended maturities:* The full amount of the debt services being renegotiated would be rescheduled, at market interest rates, with a 25-year maturity and 14-year grace period;

(c)   *Concessional interest rate:* The full amount would be rescheduled as in (b), but at the shorter term in option (a) and at an interest rate that is either 3.5 percentage points below market rates or one half of market rates, whichever yields the lesser reduction.

F. CONCLUDING REMARKS

In recent years the world economy has continued its recovery from the deep recession of the early 1980s.[13] In the developed world, recently reduced and stable interest rates, low inflation, and continued tight monetary and fiscal policies are expected to provide a stimulus to world economic growth, or at least to prevent worldwide recession. However, it has taken a longer period than expected for the recovery of the economies of the United States and many other countries.

Within the developing world, economic performance has been mixed. Many countries have succeeded in reforming their domestic policies to take advantage of the changing world economy. They have emerged with strong economic growth rates and bright prospects. However, internationally there are some problems such as the slow growth in world trade, weak export commodity prices, high government deficits, and large repayment obligations on existing external debt. These have caused some developing countries, particularly the heavily indebted oil-importing countries, to face a much bleaker outlook in terms of their economic recovery over the next few years. The recent increase in oil prices has benefited a few oil-exporting countries, while adversely affecting many other developing countries that import oil.

In the near future, financial resources for promoting social and economic development in developing countries may have to come largely from domestic savings, given the recent experience of continuing net capital outflows and the rather dim prospects for obtaining net capital inflows from developed market economies. At the same time, the difficulties associated with attracting foreign financial resources to developing countries are compounded by their huge government deficits and heavy burden of external debt.

The public sector must strengthen its role in mobilizing financial resources for promoting economic development. The present tightening of monetary policies and prudent fiscal policies pursued by many countries must be further strengthened. This tightened monetary condition has played a central role in the short-run macroeconomic performance in stabilizing and reducing interest rates and inflation. In terms of fiscal policies, means should be found to strengthen tax systems, to generate a financial surplus from public enterprises, and to reduce government subsidies. Government current expenditures should also be scrutinized with a view to reducing government deficits, generating greater government savings, and diverting them toward investment.

In both the developed market economies and the developing countries, the most important source of domestic financial resources is household savings. The government and the public enterprises typically generate deficits. It is the household sector that generates a surplus, thus providing a source for financing the deficits of the government and the public enterprises.

Policy actions should be geared toward increasing domestic household savings, not through a reduction in the absolute level of consumption but through measures that increase marginal savings out of growing real income. These savings should then be channeled effectively to more productive investments. This basic approach is generally well recognized. However, the question remains as to what policy measures are appropriate in each particular case. This depends, to a large extent, on the institutional factors as well as the economic environment in each individual country. For instance, a tax reduction policy that is designed to increase savings may have ambiguous results. Empirical evidence from developed countries indicates that tax incentives have not been very successful in raising the volume of savings. But the empirical answer to this question has not been well established for developing countries. However, there are a number of successful and indisputable policies that can be adopted for generating domestic savings. These include policy measures for widening and deepening the geographical and functional scope of the banking system; the establishment of complementarities among commercial banks, cooperative banks, and moneylenders in informal markets; more effective management of informal and formal savings deposit institutions in rural and remote areas; development of secure, attractive, and inexpensive deposit instruments; and establishment of a structure of positive real interest rates.

NOTES

1. The chapter is a revision of a paper by Wuu-Long Lin, "Trends and Structural Change in the Financial Resources of the Public Sector with Special Focus on Developing Countries," *The Role of the Public Sector in Promoting the Economic Development of Developing Countries,* United Nations, DDSMS/SFM, 94/2 (New York, 1994). pp. 51-78.

2. For discussion on taxation, disincentives, and distortions, see Peter Saunders and Friedrich Klau, *The Role of the Public Sector,* OECD Economics Studies no. 4 (Paris: OECD, 1985), pp. 160-188.

3. The World Bank, *World Development Report 1988* (Oxford University Press, 1988), pp. 79-104.

4. One major classification of central government expenditure is by economic functions, that is, capital spending versus current expenditure. Capital spending as a ratio of total government outlay is about 5 percent in developed market economies based on grouping average in recent years. The remainder is for current expenditure. The point to be emphasized here is that the brunt of structural adjustment was borne by capital expenditure and thus would have a severe impact on the economy. The hard-pressed Western Hemisphere region of developing countries had to cut capital expenditure by as much as 7 percentage points to a mere 10 percent outlay in a span of five years. Many countries of Africa cut between one third and one half of the share of capital investment in total government outlay. However, for countries in the Asian region and the Middle East the capital expenditure as a ratio of total government outlay was virtually unchanged.

5. Stanley Please, "Saving Through Taxation -- Reality or Mirage?" *Finance and Development,* Vol. 4, no. 1 (March 1967): pp. 24-32; Stanley Please, "The 'Please Effect' Revisited," World Bank Working Paper no. 82, 1970.

6. For a detailed discussion of financing and debt in developing countries, see International Monetary Fund, *World Economic Outlook* (Washington, D.C., 1989), pp. 19-29.

7. For a discussion on budget deficits and the crowding-out effect, see Saunders and Klau, *The Role of the Public Sector,* pp.168-188.

8. In the case of industrial countries, tightening of monetary conditions began in 1987 and monetary policy has assumed a central role in short-run microeconomic management. Though with sharp increases in short-term interest rates, long-term interest rates remained remarkably stable in most countries in recent years. However, fiscal policy made less progress toward medium-term consolidation. In particular, the federal budget deficit of the United States widened. However, Japan is making further progress toward fiscal consolidation. For the smaller industrial countries taken as a group, fiscal policy is expected to continue to have a restrictive impact on public expenditure.

9. The United States is the country with the largest absolute amount of foreign debt.

Total U.S. government debt was $4.035 trillion in September 1992, about 78 percent of GDP, and government deficit was $400 billion in 1992, 37 percent of total receipts. However, the U.S. is not a country with debt-servicing difficulties, but concern has arisen about the sustainability of the growth given its net foreign debtor position. Germany and Japan are the countries with the largest net sources of finance.

10. The developing countries used to be net capital importers. In each year since 1983, some developing countries became net capital exporters to the rest of the world. The net transfer of financial resources of the capital-importing countries based on a sample of 98 countries increased from US-$0.7 billion in 1983 to -$32.5 billion in 1988. See United Nations, *World Economic Survey 1989* United Nations publication Sales No. E.89.II.C.1 (1989), p. 63.

11. Chronologically, the Baker plan was introduced in September 1985. It involved intensification of economic reforms in the debtor countries, coupled with a redoubled effort to mobilize concerted loans for them from commercial banks and official leaders. Since the Baker plan was not supported by the commercial banks, the market menu approach emerged in 1987. In 1989, the Brady plan was introduced. For a complete analysis of the evolution of the official debt management strategy and the emergence of the market menu approach see "The Evolution of the External Debt Problem in Latin America and in the Caribbean," Estudios e Informes de la CEPAL No. 72, United Nations publications Sales No. E.88.II.G.10. 1988.

12. Cited from United Nations, *World Economic Survey 1989,* p. 68.

13. The slackened economic growth in the developing world in the 1970s and 1980s was caused, among others, by exogeneous factors such as deterioration in terms of trade, crop failures in many parts of the world in 1972-1975, sudden and sharp rises in oil prices in 1973 and again in 1979-1980, sharp declines in food output due to severe drought in Sub-Saharan Africa in the early 1980s, and recession in the developed countries in the 1970s and again during 1981-1983.

Chapter 7

CONTROL AND MANAGEMENT OF PUBLIC EXPENDITURE

A. INTRODUCTION

A.1 Growing Concern About Out of Control Public Expenditure

Of the concerns on financial management presented in the preceding two chapters the most prominent issue is control and management of public expenditure.[1] The need for rigorous expenditure control has arisen from the frequent and almost regular occurrence of government overspending. These excesses of expenditure over approved estimates have caused considerable public concern and undermined confidence in the integrity of government. Every dollar of budget deficit adds a dollar to debt and it is unlikely that the public debt in many countries can be reduced substantially by raising taxes much beyond their present level. Thus, more effective control of public expenditure becomes necessary.

Moreover, curtailing public expenditure corresponds with the view that the rising share of public expenditure in total national expenditure has contributed to the deterioration in the economic performance of the market economies since the mid-1970s. The so-called crowding-out effect discussed in Section D.3 of Chapter 6 refers to the fall in private consumption or investment as a result of a rise in government expenditure, thus causing the deterioration of the economy.

In times of economic austerity, governments are often faced with declining revenues together with political constraints on increasing taxes. Different governments have different views about the proper size of public expenditure, but all have the same task of reconciling it with government revenue.

A.2   Faster Growth in Public Expenditure than in GDP

In Table 7.1, the growth rate of public consumption is compared with that of GDP for a large number of developing countries. It appears from this table that a higher proportion of countries were successful in keeping their public consumption growth no higher than GDP growth in the period 1980-1990 than in periods 1965-1973 and 1973-1983. The contrast in pattern is presented in the following:

(a)   *1965-1973 and 1973-1983:* During the period 1973-1983, a bigger proportion of countries, that is 45 of 65 countries, showed faster growth in public consumption than in GDP, with the remaining 20 countries showing the opposite. In 40 of these 45 countries, GDP was increasing; in the remaining five countries it was decreasing. Tabulation of earlier data for the period 1965-1973 reveals a similar pattern to that of 1973-1983, although the numbers of countries in each category are not identical.

(b)   *1980-1990:* During the period 1980-1990, less than one half of countries, that is, 37 of 76 countries, showed faster growth of public consumption than of GDP; the remaining 39 countries showed the opposite pattern.

Although the statistics presented in Table 7.1 omit important parts of government expenditures, notably capital outlays, transfer payments and subsidies, interest payments, and net lending, they shed some light on the fiscal problems that some developing countries experienced during the periods under examination. The demand for public goods and services in many developing countries caused government expenditure to grow at a faster rate than national income in any of the three periods mentioned. In the period between 1980 and 1990, five countries showed faster growth of public consumption than that of GDP even in the time of decreasing GDP growth.

The following discussion focuses on three areas: the nature and causes of the current problems, means and techniques of controlling public current expenditures, and selected countries' experiences.

B.   THE NATURE AND CAUSES OF CURRENT PROBLEMS

B.1   The Determinants of Public Expenditure Growth

Table 7.2 presents a list of a number of important political, economic, and sociodemographic factors accounting for the upward trend in public expenditure. This list is by no means exhaustive but represents the factors common to most countries with differing emphasis. Some of these are briefly considered here under three headings: political and institutional, economic, and sociodemographic factors.

Table 7.1
Annual Growth Rate of Public Consumption Compared with Gross Domestic Product, Developing Countries, 1965–1973, 1973–1983, and 1980–1990

		Numbers of countries[a]		
		1965-1973	1973-1983	1980-1990
1.	Public consumption was increasing more rapidly than GDP			
	GDP was increasing	38	40	34
	GDP was decreasing	1	5	3
	Sum	39	45	37
2.	Public consumption was increasing at the same rate or less rapidly than GDP			
	GDP was increasing	26	20	34
	GDP was decreasing	0	0	5
	Sum	26	20	39
3.	Total number of countries			
	GDP was increasing	64	60	68
	GDP was decreasing	1	5	8
	Sum	65	65	76

[a] Although the total number of countries is coincidentally the same, the countries are not identical in each of the periods, 1965-1973 and 1973-1983. Also the countries in the above mentioned two periods are not identical with that of the period 1980-1990.

Source: Tabulated from World Bank, *World Development Report 1985* New York, Oxford University Press (1985), pp. 176 – 177 and 180 – 181.*World Development Report 1992,* pp. 220 – 221 and 232 – 233.

Table 7.2
A List of Factors Affecting the Determinants of Public Expenditure

Political and institutional factors	Economic factors	Socio-demographic factors
1. National defense and war	1. Keynesian revolution in the role of public finance and its relation to national planning.	1. Social justice, broad based welfare systems and national policy on income redistribution intended to ensure a minimum level of income and reasonable access to all essential services such as medical care, social security, education.
2. International demonstration effect, such as arms race, upgrading of public services to achieve the same standard as other countries.	2. Acceptance of deficit financing and increasing tolerance of public debt and taxation.	2. Urbanization, significant internal migration to cities resulting in increases in public services.
3. Enlarged role of Government in economic life and public services, as posited in Wagner's law.	3. Ratchet effect caused by ease of increasing but difficulty of decreasing public expenditure.	3. Population growth, changes in age structure (especially the school-age group and the elderly) and changes in population density.
4. Creation of state-owned enterprises to wrest control of key enterprises from foreign owners or minority ethnic groups, to prevent private sector bankruptcies, etc.	4. The way in which, where taxation is progressive, inflation and economic growth generate a disproportionate growth in tax revenue (fiscal drag effect) which is available for spending.	4. Enlarging responsibility of Government in conserving environment, anti-population, etc.
5. Collective pressure of politicians and ministers to maintain and improve the existing programmes.	5. Substantial increases in infrastructure investment, such as highways, water dams, raise costs of operation and maintenance.	
6. A host of interest and promotional groups and popular pressure for public goods.	6. Complementarity between the demand for public services and economic growth.	
7. Political ideology, rising expectations and the greater power of low-income groups to demand social services.	7. Price support for agricultural products, and the subsidization of infant industry.	
8. Rigidity of certain entitlement programmes and inflexibility of legislation to revise existing programmes.	8. Development of science and technology in which the Government has played an important role and where the costs are high and the risks of a kind that the private sector cannot readily take.	

(1) *Political and institutional factors:* The growth and distribution of public current expenditure are fundamentally the outcome of political decisions that result from a host of interest and promotional groups, and most importantly from politicians and their party supporters. Powerful forces have been the growth in the political power of the lower-income groups of society and the widening demand for a basic minimum level of income and reasonable access of all to essential services such as education and health. The effects of the arms race have resulted in rapidly increasing growth of defense expenditure.

(2) *Economic factors:* Increases in public spending are attributed to economic growth and are considered a means of promoting that growth. As early as in 1890, Adolph Wagner identified three main causes of this expenditure growth, Wagner's law:

(a) As a society developed and became more complex, there would be a greater need for public administration, maintenance of law and order, and regulation of economic activity;

(b) Economic growth would produce a rise in industrial monopolies that would require government control and subsequent government subsidies caused by inefficiency;

(c) There would be an increased demand for government to provide welfare and cultural activities—services for which the income elasticity of demand is greater than unity.

Economic thought was greatly influenced by the Keynesian revolution. Public expenditure and taxation were seen as instruments to be used to correct short-term cyclical fluctuation in the process of economic development and to achieve full employment. For example, in the United Kingdom, the Treasury was once charged with implementing Keynesian theory by deficit spending in times of slump. Similarly, public expenditure has been used for operation and maintenance of infrastructure such as water dams and highway, and for promotion of the development of science and technology.

(3) *Sociodemographic factors:* Current expenditure in many countries has been expanded greatly in response to social objectives and changes in the demographic structure. Social justice has always been a legitimate argument for promoting welfare programs. This is particularly true of expenditures on social security and welfare in the developed countries.

Demographic variables are equally important forces in inducing the demand for services. The following are some examples: greater demand for education due to larger share of school-age group in the population, higher demand for social security and medical care due to a larger share of the elderly population, and increased public expenditure on urban infrastructure due to urbanization.

B.2   Causes of Loss of Control

It is not always easy to identify any single factor that can explain why expenditure may go "out of control." This is often the outcome of a complex of factors that reinforce each other.

(1)   *Ratchet effect and rigidity programs:* The ratchet effect can be explained by the experience of the United Kingdom, where it has been argued that it is difficult to get a new expenditure program into the government budget, but that once in it is incorporated, it is even harder to get it out.[2] As a matter of prestige, ministers are very reluctant to make concessions that reduce the allocations to their programs, even at a time when there is a need for new programs to meet emerging issues.

In the United States, as elsewhere, certain outlays are regarded as statutory programs. They are continual expenditures that are relatively uncontrollable through the annual budget process. Such expenditures include automatic payments such as entitlements, debt services, and long-term contracts. In particular, certain individual entitlements under law lie within the jurisdiction of the House Ways and Means Committee and the Senate Finance Committee, and their amount is derived automatically from the operation of established legislative formulae.

In the developing economies, many coffee, copper, and oil-exporting countries were caught by this ratchet effect during the 1970s. They set their public spending on the basis of revenue at times when the prices of their staple exports were exceptionally high and/or export volume was high. When export revenues decreased as a result of price collapse or volume reduction, expenditure could not be easily reduced.

(2)   *Inflation:* The extent of the impact of inflation on government revenues and expenditures varies among countries, depending on their tax systems. In industrial countries, a large share of government revenue comes from income and corporation taxes and the tax system has a built-in progression. Inflation will then have the effect of moving taxpayers into higher tax brackets and overall tax revenues will then grow faster than real income. In developing countries, a large share of government revenue is derived from indirect taxes on domestic commercial transactions and international trade, and there are often considerable time lags in making tax adjustments. Consequently, these time lags produce a decline of government revenue in real terms.

In terms of government expenditure, estimates are generally adjusted by price index for such items as wages and salaries, defense items, and capital-related items. Uncertainties regarding future development make it difficult to work out a meaningful budget with an appropriate adjustment for inflation, thus resulting in either underestimation or overestimation of budgets.

(3) *Poor forecasting:* Budget estimations are derived from formulae based on a number of assumptions. In a dynamic economy, it is not an easy task to make correct assumptions in such areas as inflation, national product, expected demand for services and entitlements. This difficulty leads to poor forecasting on budgeting.

The experience of controlling public expenditure in the United Kingdom during the early 1970s revealed the difficulty of forecasting costs accurately enough for the figures to be used for purposes of control even one year ahead. As admitted by the Treasury, if the forecasting covers a period of four or five years, the figures are little better than an informed guess. Such experience applies equally to most other countries.

(4) *Supplementary appropriations and policy changes:* Supplementary appropriations are intended to meet the need for unforeseen expenditure. However, they become loopholes used to finance unexpected expenditure programs as a consequence of lobbying by interested groups. Frequently, the result is that approved funds that had a higher priority in the past are preempted or the government is forced into budget deficits.

C. GUIDELINES FOR CONTROLLING PUBLIC CURRENT EXPENDITURES

C.1 General Guidelines

Guidelines that have been developed to control public current expenditure generally follow the budget cycle of estimates, appropriation, and audit. Such guidelines are based on the same principles dercribed in the discussion of the integrated financial management process (see Sections B and D of Chapter 5) and the development planning process of formulation, implementation, and evaluation (see discussion in Chapter 3). However, the present discussions focus specifically on controlling public current expenditure.

(1) *Determination of aggregate expenditure: matching revenue with expenditure:* One important theme underlying the effective control of public expenditure is that expenditure decisions cannot be taken realistically unless the necessary resources are considered at the same time. Normal limits of total expenditure can be represented by the following equation:

Government expenditure = revenues + foreign aid + deficit

Although the principle of matching expenditure and taxation is simple, there are major difficulties in practice. There are at least two important considerations on this subject: the need for long-term survey of expenditure and revenue (see discussion in Section D of Chapter 5) and the need for strengthening of institutional mechanisms of establishing collective ministerial responsibility for oversight of public expenditure as a whole package.

(2) *Resource allocation: value for money:* The second stage of the public expenditure process, the allocation to programs, can be regarded as a competing bid among the spending agencies and as a bargaining game between the spending agencies and the Treasury. The bargaining process involves a number of back-and-forth negotiations that determine who gets what and how much of government resources.

There are no standardized rules in resource allocation. In some countries, nondefense expenditure is simply treated as a remainder after defense needs have been predetermined on the basis of primarily political considerations. In most developed countries, a significant portion of total expenditure comprises entitlements, continuing charges or nonvoted expenditures, including such items as the salaries of the heads of government; the judiciary; and interest payments. Thus, fewer resources then might be thought are subject to policy reallocation. Similarly, most developing countries have few resources subject to policy reallocation since their limited resources are obligated to continue expenditures such as wages and maintenance of government buildings.

"Value for money" is a common theme in budget allocation. In the General Accounting Office of the United States, measures of value for money fall into two general categories—budgetary savings and better use of funds. Budgetary savings reduce costs, and thus federal spending, through such measures as consolidated management of base support services within the same department. Better use of funds reduces costs and reallocates funds for more effective use by the agency through such measures as eliminating unnecessary reviews of all classified materials. A 1983 United States report noted that the work of the General Accounting Office had identified over US$1.7 billion in budgetary savings and over $2.7 billion in better use of funds.

(3) *Budget in action: portfolio cash management:* Most governments find it necessary to have an annual budget, even though a coherent program requires budgeting over a much longer period. An annual budget provides a detailed breakdown not only of planned expenditures but also of receipts from various taxes and other sources. It deals with the availability and commitment of funds and the regularity of financial control. It is a useful tool for checking budgetary balance and providing data for financial management. There is a need for a certain amount of budget flexibility to be able to meet the needs of unforeseen changes such as inflation and export earnings, although an annual budget often takes the form of "block appropriations" with respect to government plans and programs in a given fiscal year.

More countries have begun to focus on sound practices of cash management, since cash flow dictates the ability to carry out planned programs regardless of whether they are budgeted. One primary goal of effective cash management is to make cash available when needed, thereby minimizing the interest incurred on debt. Cash management requires, among other things, assessment of the seasonality of revenues and expenditures, advance information about the pattern and timing of expenditure, forecasts of cash requirements, and appropriation of accounts, program by program.

Cash management concerns itself not only with money availability and avoidance of overspending but also with prevention of rush spending at the end of the fiscal year. In assessing budget implementation for the Zambian economy, for instance, it was found that the problem of the "end-of-the-year" rush spending in 1973 was more or less the same as in the previous years, that is, with as much as one third of the total authorized expenditure left to be spent in the last month of the year. To prevent this outcome, most countries adopt portfolio management of liquidity, by which means the timing of cash releases is synchronized with the fulfillment of commitments. In the case of the United States, Congress has legislated that the last quarter expenditures may not be more than 20 percent of the total budget.

(4)   *Postbudget evaluation.* The scope of postbudget evaluation is discussed in Section E of Chapter 3 on plan evaluation. In short, the main objectives of budget evaluation are the achievement of plan targets, contribution to national development, reasonable costs, and compliance with laws and regulations.

One point to be emphasized here is the complementarity of external and internal evaluators. On the one hand, external evaluators are usually respected for their objective viewpoint. But the so-called outside inspectors may not have as full an understanding of the issues as those who implement the program, thus causing misinterpretations. On the other hand, the so-called built-in evaluation by internal evaluators can enforce responsibility for project activities from the very beginning and take remedial actions in time. But those who are associated with the program from the beginning are naturally somewhat disinclined to admit their own mistakes.

C.2   Macroeconomic Aspects of Expenditure Control

On the basis of these guidelines, one can generalize the major macroeconomic aspects of expenditure control as follows:

(a)   *The need to examine all expenditures together:* All expenditures must be reviewed as a whole package.

(b)   *The need to look beyond a year:* A long-term financial survey serves as the basis for synchronizing annual expenditure. This is particularly relevant to most capital projects, which take much more than one year to complete, and expenditure on education and pensions, which can be easily projected.

(c)   *The need to have regard for resource constraints:* Prospective resources such as expected growth of national products and external aid/loan should be assessed periodically.

(d)   *The need to consider tax expenditures:* Tax expenditure is the reduction of tax liability in such items as reliefs, concessions, and exemptions provided through the tax system. Their advantages must be weighed against costs.

(e)   *Early warnings, financial information, and cash limits:* In a world of uncertain and rapidly changing economic conditions, a financial information system will help in controlling expenditure through provision of early warnings and cash limits.

(f)   *The need for monitoring:* Periodic monitoring can assess problems encountered in management of public expenditure, so that remedial measures may be taken in time.

C.3   Microaspects of Public Expenditure Control

In terms of the guidelines developed in Section C.1, one can generalize some microaspects of public expenditure control as follows:

(a)   *Motivation and responsibility:* Success in management of public expenditure as well as in any kind of management requires clarification of responsibility and provision of incentives to efficiency. Staff motivation through such measures as salary increase and promotions can reinforce their responsibilities in performing duties.

(b)   *Cost of using quantitative techniques:* Techniques used for project assessment should equally weigh both cost and benefit. A simple and easy to understand technique is particularly desirable in developing countries.

(c)   *Training and personnel:* Well-trained personnel are essential to good performance, and appropriate compensation to personnel is essential to their commitment to their work.

(d)   *Financial information:* A flow of updated financial information is a necessary key to successful financial management. Personal computers equipped with large core capacity at an affordable price are good tools to assist efficient financial management.

(e)   *Objectives, performance indicators, and quality:* Effective management requires a clarification of objectives and performance indicators. Performance evaluation should include some forms of quality check.

(f)   *External review:* In addition to a built-in evaluation by internal review, independent external review can promote efficiency in project implementation. Generally, external evaluators may be in a better position to give an objective view of performance.

D. SELECTED COUNTRIES' EXPERIENCES

There is no wholly scientific way to control public expenditure and receipts. Any control is a mixture of politics, economics, and experience in public management. Measures and techniques used for the management and control of public expenditure must accommodate different economic administrative settings, which vary among countries and change over time within a country.

The following observations are intended to highlight alternative methods that have been adopted by selected countries with varying degrees of success and to provide indications of lessons learned.

D.1   Developed Market Economies

(1)   In the United States, Congress in the past authorized funds through a patchwork of appropriation bills and did not have strong machinery for overall budgetary control and coordination.

In order to gain budgetary control, Congress enacted the Congressional Budget and Impoundment Control Act of 1974. This act restricted the president's ability to impound funds. It also established the foundation of the current system, whereby Congress annually examines and approves presidential spending plans. Essentially, this act took three forms:

(a)   The act imposed a strict timetable on all the budgetary processes to be processed by both the executive branch and the legislature.

(b)   The act established new budget committees in each House of Congress, charged with performing a task of integration. All congressional committees were required to work within the targets and ceilings of spending set by the budget committee.

(c)   The act established a new information agency, the Congressional Budget Office, to assist Congress in its control of finances. The purpose of the Congressional Budget Office is to provide an independent assessment of the state of the economy and of national needs, which can be set against that of the executive.

However, this act does not have a mandate for budget balance.[3] In terms of an annual federal deficit as a ratio of total receipts, there is no consistent pattern. The result is that the deficit increased from 14 percent in 1980 to a peak of 35 percent in 1983, then decreased to a low of 15 percent in 1989, and finally increased to its highest peak of 37 percent in 1992.

(2)   In the United Kingdom, the Public Expenditure Survey Committee was established to implement the recommendations of the 1961 Plowden Committee. The committee provides a forum for government departments and the Treasury to evaluate existing and planning expenditure programs and their implications for the economy as a whole. One of the committee's tasks is to coordinate the pattern and overall growth of public expenditure over a period of years in the light of a medium-term economic analysis and to provide the data for the purpose of expenditure control.

However, the committee failed to control overspending. The government's reaction was to supplement the Public Expenditure Survey Committee with a system of cash limits and a new financial information system.

(a)   *Cash limits:* In an effort to control increasing levels of actual public expenditure, a system of cash limits introduced in 1976 took the form of specified maximum amounts of cash to be spent on certain services or blocks of services in the coming year. They covered some two thirds of central government expenditure, the main exception being demand-determined expenditures such as unemployment pay and retirement pensions.

(b)   *A warning system:* A new financial information system was installed in the Treasury. Each spending department was required to submit returns of expenditure to the Treasury within ten working days of the end of each month. This enabled the Treasury to monitor the monthly expenditure and to investigate discrepancies.

Although the changes have removed the deficiencies of the Public Expenditure Survey Committee System, there was no built-in mechanism to prevent budget deficit. Governments seeking to cut or moderate expenditure are likely to promise future reductions, which do not materialize because of an overoptimistic assumption of the growth of the national economy. Also, the effectiveness of cash limits is dependent on accurate forecasting of the rate of inflation. Unfortunately, inaccurate forecasting has led to frequent revision of inflation rates and cash limits. Frequent revision of cash limits can undermine the credibility of the system.

D.2 Developing Economies

Developing economies have been strongly urged to reduce expenditure through stricter management of public expenditure, in particular by cutting subsidies to public enterprises, maintaining tighter control of public sector wages, and lowering military spending.

The following are selected countries' experiences:

(a)   As pioneered by the experience of industrial countries such as the United Kingdom and France, many developing countries have been divesting themselves of state-owned enterprises ownership in an effort to improve efficiency and competition. Such countries include Bangladesh, Chile, Kenya, Malaysia, Mexico, the Philippines, Thailand, Togo, and Turkey.[4] Policy initiatives in this context were implemented through various measures of liquidation, privatization of ownership, and privatization of management.

(b)   Different measures have been taken by countries to control the wage bill in the public sector. For instance, "ghost" workers who received government wages but were not employed in the government were eliminated in the Central African Republic and Guinea. Temporary positions were eliminated in Gambia and Jamaica. Automatic and voluntary retirements were imposed in Costa Rica and Senegal. An across-the-board wage cut was introduced in Togo.[5]

(c)   Commodity booms and busts have had a negative impact on export earnings from primary commodities in Africa, causing painful fluctuations in public expenditure. In Botswana, a system was introduced to prevent excessive increases in public expenditure during the boom periods and to build international reserves and balances at the central bank to be used at the end of the boom period.[6]

(d)   In Sierra Leone, in addition to quarterly ceilings, which are sometimes issued as austerity measures, expenditure control is built into the accounting system in various ways. One regulation imposes an obligation on vote controllers (delegated by the head of each ministry/department) to keep vote service ledgers in a manner that shows a true picture of the position of the various votes before an item of expenditure is processed. These rules impose personal and pecuniary responsibility on the vote controllers for any overexpenditures incurred in their votes.

NOTES

1. The major reference for this chapter is a report drafted by Wuu-Long Lin for a United Nations publication, *Planning and Control of Public Current Expenditure: Lessons of Country Experience,* United Nations publication Sales No. E.87.II.H.3 (1987).

2. Maurice Wright, "Public Expenditure in Britain: The Crises of Control," *Public Administration* 55 (Summer 1977): pp. 143-169.

3. Although the Gramm-Rudman-Hollings law was eventually ruled unconstitutional, it provides a striking illustration of the relationship between Congress and the executive in relation to budget balance. Between 1980 and 1986 the total federal debt of the United States increased from about 35 percent of GNP to nearly 50 percent; interest payments rose from 9 to about 15 percent of the budget. Growing concern about the potentially detrimental impact of federal budget deficits on the economy led to a call for a balanced budget. With this in view, the Gramm-Rudman-Hollings law -- the Balanced Budget and Emergency Deficit Control Act of 1985, Public Law 99-177 -- was passed. It was designed to balance the federal budget by providing for automatic across-the-board cuts if a specific schedule of reductions were not met. Under the law, Congress delegated power to the Comptroller General, who heads the General Accounting Office, to certify the level of mandatory deficit reduction cuts. However, in July 1986 the law was ruled unconstitutional by the Supreme Court on the grounds that it violated the constitutional principle of the separation of powers by vesting executive branch authority in a legislative branch official.

4. See World Bank, *World Development Report 1987* (New York: Oxford University Press, 1987), p. 68.

5. For a more detailed discussion, see World Bank, *World Development Report 1988* (New York: Oxford University Press, 1988), pp. 116-117.

6. See World Bank, Sub-Saharan Africa – From Crisis to Sustainable Growth (Washington, D.C., 1989), p. 167.

Part III

ENTERPRISE MANAGEMENT AND TECHNOLOGY DEVELOPMENT

Both employment creation and increases in productivity are major development objectives for promoting economic development. Better enterprise management in both the public and private sectors and adaptation of appropriate technology are essential elements of a successful development strategy.

The following discussions include three chapters. Chapter 8 discusses management and privatization of public enterprises, and Chapter 9 discusses entrepreneurship and development of small and medium enterprises. The subject of transfer and development of science and technology is discussed in Chapter 10.

Chapter 8

MANAGEMENT AND PRIVATIZATION OF PUBLIC ENTERPRISES

A. EMERGING ISSUES

Besides the centrally planned economies, most governments in developing countries and some governments in developed market countries created and promoted public enterprises between the mid-1960s and the early 1980s. Public enterprises were created for many reasons. They were used as instruments for public revenue generation, job creation, and promotion of socioeconomic development, which were particularly important in the economies in which the private sector was considered to be weak and ineffective and private investment was inadequate.

Unfortunately, the public enterprise sector came under more serious scrutiny and pressure for reform in the late 1980s and the beginning of the 1990s than at any other time in development history. Its performance was generally condemned as unsatisfactory, although there were some exceptions. Politicians and taxpayers can no longer tolerate the continuing and enlarging tax burdens to finance the burgeoning financial losses of public enterprises.

A.1 Burgeoning Deficits in Public Enterprises

According to a World Bank report on a limited sample of 11 developing countries,[1] public enterprises have made large and growing claims on the government budget. There are, however, substantial intercountry differences in terms of both the absolute size and the rate of change. Of these 11 countries, the budgetary net claims of nonfinancial state-owned enterprises as a percentage of GDP at market prices were highest in Sri Lanka and Zambia. This ratio was as high as about 11 percent in Sri Lanka in 1978-1980, having increased 7 percentage points since 1966-1969. This ratio was slightly more than 10 percent in Zambia in 1978-1980, having doubled since 1966-1969. Tanzania experienced the largest increase, from about 0.5 percent in 1966-1969 to above 5 percent in 1977: a tenfold increase within a decade. In contrast, India alone showed a decrease of this ratio, from slightly more than 3 percent in 1966-1969 to slightly less than 3 percent in 1981-1982.

The statistics contained in a 1984 report of the United Nations Economic and Social Commission for Asia and the Pacific (ESCAP) further illustrate the diversity of country experience in terms of the generation of financial resources by public enterprise. Table 8.1 illustrates the share of public enterprises in gross national savings, gross domestic capital formation, and the share of their savings in their own gross capital formation, for India, the Philippines, the Republic of Korea, Sri Lanka, and Thailand. They were divided into three periods during 1970-1983. At least three observations from this table are relevant to the present discussion:

(a)   With the exception of the Philippines, public enterprises in all countries experienced a much larger fraction of gross domestic formation than of national savings.

(b)   The share of public enterprises in gross national savings tended to decline while their share in gross capital formation tended to rise, though not consistently over time, in India, the Republic of Korea, and Thailand.

(c)   Public enterprise savings as a proportion of public enterprise capital formation was comparatively small and tended to decline over time for India and Thailand.

The preceding observations imply that the financing of capital formation in public enterprises relies largely on external savings or other components of domestic savings in many developing countries. Relatedly, public enterprises have run into deficits, creating sizable demands on government budgets, bank credit, and foreign borrowing.

Common weaknesses of public enterprises and their associated financial losses include several interrelated factors, such as unclear, multiple, or contradictory objectives; overly centralized decision making; excessive personnel cost; and market distortion caused by state monopolized prices.

A.2   Continuing Dominance of Public Enterprises

Despite increasing criticism of public enterprises and pressure for divestment, the public enterprise sector has not diminished by any significant extent in most developing countries. They are likely to continue to exist in most developing countries in the foreseeable future. There are various reasons for this assertion.

First, although privatization will continue to be a powerful government policy tool to solve the problems of economic inefficiency in public enterprises, this does

Table 8.1
Selected ESCAP Economies: Share of Public Enterprises (PEs) in Gross National Savings, Gross Domestic Capital Formation, and Share of Their Savings in Their Own Gross Capital Formation, 1970–1983 (Percentages)

	1970-1974[a]			1975-1979[a]			1980-1983[a]		
	Share in gross national savings	Share in gross capital formation	Share of PE savings in PE capital formation	Share in gross national savings	Share in gross capital formation	Share of PE savings in PE capital formation	Share in gross national savings	Share in gross capital formation	Share of PE savings in PE capital formation
India	2.9	31.4	8.7	4.1	38.5	11.2	2.0[b]	34.7[b]	5.6[b]
Philippines	14.7	7.8	105.0	24.7	17.9	72.8	36.7[c]	21.7[c]	81.3[c]
Republic of Korea	14.4[d]	20.5[d]	60.0[d]	13.8	21.3	49.2	9.9[e]	26.4[e]	25.4[e]
Sri Lanka	...	30.2	...	5.4[f]	29.8[f]	11.7[f]	9.9	18.8	26.4
Thailand	6.5	25.8	18.4	3.1	26.9	7.1	3.8	35.4	5.6

[a] Intercountry comparisons should not be made because of differences in coverage.
[b] 1980 only.
[c] Average of 1980-1982 only.
[d] Average of 1971-1974 only.
[e] Average of 1980-1981 only.
[f] Average of 1978-1979 only.

Source: United Nations, Economic and Social Survey of Asia and the Pacific 1984, United Nations publication, Sales No. F.85.II.F.1 (1985), p.172.

not mean that public enterprises will disappear overnight or even in the near future. With the exception of some countries, such as Bangladesh, Chile, Malaysia, Argentina, Venezuela, and Jamaica, few developing countries have succeeded in privatizing large public enterprises with substantial assets and numerous employees. Privatization has encountered a number of difficulties that cannot be easily solved by government authorities at this time, including smallness of the domestic market, absence of capital market and funds, lack of political will, and inadequate management skills. This in turn suggests that a number of public enterprises will continue to coexist with private sector entities.

Second, not all public enterprises should or could be privatized because of their status as natural monopolies. There will continue to be a need in a large number of countries for public enterprises in basic services such as electricity, water supply, postal, and telecommunications services. Nevertheless, performance in these public enterprises could be enhanced by increasing managers' competence and strengthening their autonomy and accountability.

In view of the continuing dominance of public enterprises in the national economy and pressures for rationalization of public enterprises, two broad approaches have been adopted in varying mixes in developing countries, namely reform in public enterprise management and privatization.

B. REFORM IN PUBLIC ENTERPRISES MANAGEMENT

Reform in public enterprises still continues to be a favored policy option because not all public enterprises can be privatized because of constraints and immediate consequences of privatization (e.g., economic dislocation and sudden unemployment).[2] Policymakers also tend to believe that in the pursuit of development policies and objectives (e.g., social justice, eradication of poverty), a reformed public enterprise sector may be a more reliable instrument than premature privatization.

The following discussion treats (1) the development of entrepreneurship in public enterprises; (2) the creation of competitive environment, autonomy, and decentralized management; and (3) human resources development.

B.1 Development of Entrepreneurship in Public Enterprises

Entrepreneurial development, which emerged in the 1980s, is increasingly taking place in the private sector (a subject to be discussed further in Chapter 9). However, despite apparent incompatibility in terms of ownership and objectives, public enterprises can, both in principle and in practice, adopt major entrepreneurial methods and instruments in their operation and management.

Barriers that impede the development and practice of entrepreneurship in public enterprise can be identified. First, severe constraints to efficiency in public enterprises and corresponding impediments to entrepreneurship arise from government control, budget limitations, and bureaucratic organizational structure. Also, governments have traditionally viewed public enterprises as an instrument for achieving not only commercial but also social objectives. This social element is often unfavorable to the development of entrepreneurship.

The development of entrepreneurship in public enterprises can proceed in the following two forms:

(a) The entry of new enterprises will increase the competitiveness of existing public enterprises. New enterprises will challenge existing firms, seek market shares, and adopt new technology. In turn, this will create an environment that induces entrepreneurship in the existing public enterprises. In this regard, existing laws and regulations that restrict entry of new firms in most developing and socialist countries, in particular, should be amended appropriately. Such an amendment is particularly needed in many socialist countries, where entry of new enterprises was practically impossible and private enterprise was generally limited to a few employees.

(b) Entrepreneurship within public enterprises can be developed to transform existing public enterprises, facilitating their entry into new dimensions of competition. Under the umbrella of an organization, numerous small entrepreneurial groups interact and venture into invention of new technology and application of new production and marketing opportunities. Public enterprises can use their incumbent economic and financial advantages to cultivate incubators of entrepreneurial activity.

Furthermore, public enterprises can play an active role in the promotion of indigenous entrepreneurship in the future. For instance, they can offer consultancy, technical and financial assistance, and subcontracts to newly created private enterprises that will interact with the incubators in the public sector.

B.2 Creation of a Competitive Environment

To develop entrepreneurship in public enterprises requires a competitive environment. The creation of a competitive environment requires the existence of more firms in the market. A competitive market structure could be attained by (a) entry of new firms and (b) development of incubators within existing public enterprises firms.

First, promotion of competition cannot be simply accomplished by repeal of the statutory monopoly status of a public enterprise. The experience of the United Kingdom illustrates that the public sector electricity industry has the incumbent endowment of technical and financial advantages, and this is likely either to deter entry or to make the experience of entrants unattractive. The financial strength that arises from its monopoly in a larger market for electricity supply provides the resources to cross-subsidize its continued presence in the electrical appliance retailing market.

Ideally, creation of competitive environment could be achieved by the adoption of the following policies[3]:

✓ Absence of governmental barriers to entry
   Competitive industry structure
   Equal access to loans and credit
   Equal access to foreign exchange
   Equal application of all laws
   Fair enforcement of contracts
✓ Absence of price controls or subsidies
   Equal access to raw materials and supplies
   Equal access to markets
   Equal application of laws concerning hiring and firing of employees
   Freedom to reorganize and change business within broad objectives
✓ Absence of preferential protectionism

Second, in the case of natural monopolies such as power and water, the policy measures mentioned may not all be equally applicable. Nevertheless, a principle can possibly be established to create a competitive environment in these particular enterprises. The main device behind this basic principle will be to establish norms of operation for effectiveness and efficiency. Such norms can be used as criteria for comparison of operation among various enterprises and their changes over time within the same enterprise so as to induce and stimulate a competitive spirit in the management to attain or even exceed such norms. These norms can also be used to monitor and evaluate those public enterprises with poor performance, which is sometimes due to defective and inadequate project formulation and inappropriate technology choice.

When an enterprise requires subsidies on infant industry grounds, such subsidies should be progressively reduced within a planned time frame. This would gradually increase the intensity of the competition and finally help them reach an established norm of effectiveness and efficiency.

Third, in addition to creating a competitive environment through free entry of more firms, another unique approach is the so-called incubator, which has been commonly adopted in big private corporations. A new venture under the leadership of a skilled and motivated manager is granted autonomy and nurtured within the public enterprise. The parent enterprise provides these venture activities with necessary services and supports until they mature and are ready to enter the competitive business environment. New ventures of this nature could create a competitive environment that would in turn stimulate better performance in the existing public enterprise and provide competition for private enterprises.

In Agrocombinat Slusovice Cooperative Farm (ASCF) of former Czechoslovakia, economic autonomy is granted to each organizational unit – sector, plant, workshop, down to the work collectives. Entrepreneurship is developed by each organizational unit within the enterprise. Each organizational unit purchases from and sells products to other units of the ASCF, each of which is responsible for its own economic performance. This creates a competitive environment for all organizational units to improve their management standards.

B.3   Autonomy and Decentralized Management

Inefficient management in public enterprises is often caused by the fact that managers cannot legitimately claim autonomy under the law: Many groups claim the exclusive right to decision making, including the manager, the board, the administrative ministry, the Treasury, and even the unions. Frequently, routine management is interfered with by these interest groups, thereby preventing managers from making decisions in such critical areas as product design, marketing and distribution, product pricing, financial resource mobilization and allocation, and retention of profits for capital improvement.

In a recent reform of the Algerian public enterprise system, the state has completely withdrawn from the management of public enterprises. The public enterprises are free and autonomous to make their own choice of management style, develop strategies, and make economic, financial, and personnel decisions. Enterprises naturally are developed in order to make profit; otherwise, they face the danger of bankruptcy. Implementation of such a measure has stirred workers' spirits and improved the marketing system. Further, the managers have been urged to introduce an efficient and flexible organization consisting of autonomous units under their coordination.

Another outstanding case in point is China, which after 1978 initiated various policy measures on decentralization by giving greater authority for decision making in day-to-day operation to managers at the state and local collective enterprise levels. The wage bill (including bonuses and salaries) is tied with profit share to the state. The granting of financial incentives to individual state enterprises and the operation on a semiautonomous basis in accordance with commercial principles guided by the profit motive are expected to serve as an effective means of generating a higher rate of financial surpluses. But the system has not brought about the expected goals for reasons that are not clear but probably include the government's continuing interference.

There are a number of specific instances in other countries where public enterprises, freed from government administrative and regulatory dominance, have demonstrated a capacity to compete effectively (e.g., Ethiopian Airlines and Egypt's Suez Canal Company). In these cases the respective governments have allowed autonomy in enterprise management while simultaneously requiring accountability.

The prevailing global trend toward decentralization of decision making can be seen as a step toward the creation of an environment conducive to effective and efficient management. The traditional management of hierarchical organization structure and its centralized bureaucratic control are becoming a major source of declining competitiveness. When the organizational structure is flatter and less hierarchical, this will allow individual business units to have management control of their own operation. With such decentralized management, it is possible to achieve competition among various units. For instance, although the networks of power, water, and railway transport need to be centrally planned and established, the management responsibility for their operation can be decentralized through the creation of regional monopolies. Management will be improved through this regional competition so as to attain results similar to those of the best performer.

Various forms of autonomy structure have been adopted by different countries as a means of fostering efficient management. In Yugoslavia, the self management system was first introduced in a tannery and skin-processing factory with the establishment of workers' councils. Each workers' council has management autonomy, and management of all workers' councils is coordinated by the central workers' council. In the United Kingdom, management buy-outs were introduced to transfer all or portions of ownership of public enterprises to managers/workers. The financial commitment of employees who are expecting long term returns naturally creates an environment conducive to productive activities under a strong management team.

B.4   Human Resources Development

Management skills can be fostered through educational institutions, and management talent can be supported by a proper training program. In developing economies, and particularly in centrally planned economies that are faced with a lack of management skills, the role of formal education is of great importance in the transformation process. The educational system can provide not only technical skills, but most importantly management skills, tactical strategies for innovation and change, and self-development.

Public support of a management training network can be illustrated from the experience of the United States. The Small Business Administration in collaboration with universities and business development institutions periodically conducts a series of training programs on entrepreneurial know-how. This public support program aims to reduce the failure rate among entrepreneurs who lack knowledge, for example, of new business ventures and of competition and innovation. Reduction of the high failure rate among new businesses is not only helpful to individuals starting businesses, but beneficial to the society.

Finally, international development assistance could provide experience and expertise to public enterprises attempting to foster effective management in the public sector. Such assistance could take various forms, including training programs, seminars, establishment of a network for exchange of country experience, and publications. In this regard, the United Nations Department for Development

Support and Management Services as well as other United Nations agencies have continued their past efforts to foster effective management through technical assistance, seminars, and publications. Similarly, the United Nations Development Program, the World Bank, and the International Labour Organization are assisting developing countries as well as socialist countries in various areas of effective management, such as vocational training, enterprise creation, inclusion of women in development programs, and provision of financial aid.

C. PRIVATIZATION

Privatization policies have been and will continue to be a global trend. It is estimated that more than 2,000 state-owned public enterprises have been privatized in developing countries and 6,000 worldwide since 1980. Over 80 developing countries have been involved in these efforts. Below are some of the highlights.

(a) Massive privatization programs were pioneered in the United Kingdom and France and then in Japan and other major industrial countries.

(b) Bangladesh and Chile implemented reprivatization of enterprises that had been nationalized by previous administrations.

(c) Since 1984, Mexico has sold or liquidated over a third of its 1,155 state-owned enterprises. Chile has privatized all but 23 of the 524 state-owned enterprises it had in 1973. Some other developing economies, such as those of Argentina, Jamaica, and Turkey, have undertaken significant privatization activities.

(d) Similarly, all Eastern European countries and the former Soviet Union have been undertaking an extraordinary campaign of privatization in recent years.

(e) Countries such as China, Tanzania, and Algeria, traditionally among the most favorable to a strong state role in the economy, have been contemplating some forms of privatization.

C.1 Objectives

Privatization of public enterprises typically has several interrelated objectives:

(a) *Fiscal gains:* The most practical aspect of privatization is the elimination or reduction of the debt burden as well as the budgetary deficit by disposing of loss-making enterprises.

(b) *Economic efficiency:* This includes both allocative efficiency and productive efficiency. The former refers to more efficient allocation of resources through elimination of state monopoly and increase in market competition; and the latter refers to more optimal use of inputs within the firm through elimination of government subsidies and tax exemptions.

(c)   *Private sector's spirit:* Though it is not a primary objective, an accompanying objective of privatization is to create a vibrant private sector and to increase its role in the economy.

C.2   Criteria for Selecting Public Enterprises for Privatization

The general criteria for selecting public enterprises for privatization can be classified into three broad groups: economic, administrative, and welfare considerations.

(a)   *Economic criteria:* Public enterprises with essentially commercial functions can be easily privatized since they are likely to appeal to private investors. Examples include commercial and retail trade (such as airlines and hotels) and manufacturing (such as textiles and food processing). On the other hand, public enterprises with essentially noncommercial functions are generally the problematic ones for divestiture. This generally refers to the natural monopoly sector such as public utilities and railways; one cannot simply transfer it from a public sector to a private sector monopoly.

(b)   *Administrative criteria:* Privatization is a recent adventure in the history of economic development. All countries proceed in a cautious manner since they have limited experience and administrative capacity. Other-country experience, even if successful, cannot simply be adopted because of differences in economic and political environments.

Some countries have adopted a "step-by-step" or "learning-by-doing" approach. In the United Kingdom, for instance, experience gained from the privatization of some big enterprises such as British Airways and British Steel helped them proceed in the privatization of other firms with more complicated operations. Some other countries took the risk of tackling the largest and most complex public enterprises at the outset of the privatization programs, which claimed a greater share of government budget and was used by the government to demonstrate its commitment to privatization. It is noted, however, that a massive and unplanned privatization can disrupt the existing distribution system and create new economic problems, as evidenced by experience in many Eastern European countries and the former Soviet Union.

(c)   *Welfare considerations:* Some public enterprises are not commercially profitable and are not readily subject to privatization because of their provision of social services to poor segments of the population, such as public transportation, education, and health. For instance, public transportation in Rome could not be easily privatized because it is the public view that government is obliged to subsidize public transportation and to provide cheap fares to the general public. In China, privatization of all public enterprises is not practical at the present time since the private sector is not strong enough to absorb all the labor forces.

C.3   Methods of Privatization

Privatization as defined in this book includes a full or partial sale of ownership of state-owned enterprises to the private sector and/or a partial privatization in terms of such arrangements as the management, leasing, and franchising arrangements between a state-owned enterprise and the private sector. In this regard, privatization can take a variety of forms. In the case of the United Kingdom, the number of privatization methods has exceeded twenty.

The choice of methods depends, to a large extent, on privatization objectives and the national environment. Privatization objectives could include one or a combination of the following: relief from financial burden, revenue raise, job creation, efficiency and productivity increase, foreign investment attraction, and others. These objectives have to be tailored to the specific environment of the state-owned enterprises and the social, political, and economic conditions of the country.

In the present discussion, methods of privatization are classified into nine broad categories.[4] Six of these are on transactional techniques: public offering, private placement, management/employee buyout, lease and management contract, sale of assets, and joint venture. The remaining three are nontransactional techniques: give away, liquidation/attrition, and demonopolization.

Each of these methods will be briefly presented:

(a)   *Public offering of shares:* This is a sale of state-owned enterprises to the general public through an organized market such as a stock exchange. This method was adopted in the case of British Telecom, Kenya Commercial Bank, and many other enterprises, in Chile, Hungary, and Jamaica. One advantage is that price is dictated by the market. However, public offering of shares posed a transaction problem in a situation with no established or underdeveloped capital market in countries such as Poland and former Czechoslovakia. In such a situation, an alternative method is the sale of public enterprises through other popular institutions, such as banks and post offices, as in the Jamaican sale of the National Commercial Bank.

(b)   *Private placement:* Private placement is a sale of state-owned enterprises to an entity or entities at prices determined through competitive bidding or negotiation. According to Privatization International, more than 50 percent of the privatizations in 1990 were through private sales. Examples include privatization of the telephone systems of Argentina and Mexico and the sale of the SEAT auto company in Spain to a foreign group, Volkswagen. One of its advantages is its flexibility in transactional terms, which facilitated its use as an instrument for debt swaps in order to attract foreign investors in the case of Honduras. However, it posed a problem of price determination in the absence of fair market valuations.

(c) *Management/employment buy-out:* A holding company for managers/employees is created to buy the state-owned enterprises. This method is particularly good for privatizing companies in situations when the enterprise is not easily salable and the alternative is liquidation, has competent managers, or has an employment problem. This method provides satisfaction to recipients. Good examples are the sale of one million homes to renters and the sale of British Telecom in the United Kingdom under the administration of Prime Minister Margaret Thatcher. Problems encountered include complicated negotiations about prices, credit and payment terms, and risk taking in the case of the absence of good managers.

(d) *Lease and management contracts:* The state-owned enterprise provides a contract of its management to the private sector but keeps its ownership. This method and private placement (b) appear to be used mostly in developing countries. One example is the contracting out of two fish processing plants in Nicaragua to a private firm. One obvious advantage of this method is its retention of ownership. In the case of La Union Port in El Salvador, national security interests and the constitution prevented anything beyond privatization of the management. However, in such cases government has to monitor use of the facilities closely to prevent misuse.

(e) *Sale of assets:* The transaction involves the sale of assets through competitive bidding or auction, rather than the sale of shares of a going concern. In case there are legal suits against the company on unpaid debt, it becomes necessary to separate the debt from assets, since buyers will be interested in buying the assets only, not the whole company, to avoid legal complications. An example is the sale of assets of the Pacarsa Plant in Honduras. The method is also often used as a prior step to liquidation. For instance, IRI of Italy privatized Alfa Romeo through this method by selling all of its assets of plant and trademarks to Fiat. In this transaction, it should be legally specified that the sale of the assets involved is independent of the firm's liabilities.

(f) *Joint ventures:* A private firm makes an investment in an existing state-owned enterprise, thereby diluting the government's share. This method is useful for remedying undercapitalization given the government's financial constraints. This method has been adopted by Ghana to commercialize some public enterprises. One immediate concern is to what extent the government can be restrained from political interference with management under this joint venture arrangement.

(g) *Giveaway:* This nontransactional type of privatization implies giving away the enterprise free of charge to managers, workers, or citizens at large. In the former socialist countries of Eastern Europe, firms are presumed to be collectively owned by all the people. Giving away to the people is a simple method in situations where there is no alternative of privatization given the case of no capital market, no accounting records, or no market prices. For instance, former Czechoslovakia adopted the "coupon privatization" method to auction off the state-owned enterprises, representing roughly 40 percent of the economy, among all citizens over age 18. This method solves the problems of valuation. On the negative side, citizens do not know what companies' shares are worth.

(h) *Liquidation:* Another nontransactional type of privatization is dissolving the firm. This is done in a situation where the firm is unviable and/or its equipment is relatively worthless. In Nicaragua, of the 350 state-owned enterprises for privatization, 50 were considered to be worthless and 27 were liquidated in the first year. One immediate concern regarding this method is providing "safety nets" for workers after liquidation.

(i) *Demonopolization:* It eliminates the monopoly of state-owned enterprises and opens them to market competition. In the United States, postal services are open to private firms. This strengthens efficiency through market competition.

C.4 Role of Government

The government must play an important role in privatization.[5] This is particularly necessary in developing countries where capital markets are weak or even nonexistent and the government has social and economic obligations to protect employees, small and medium enterprises, and special ethnic groups.

The following discussion highlights some measures that government can take in order to implement privatization effectively.

(a) *Public information campaign:* In the absence of financial intermediaries, the government can attract investors through mass campaigns of public information. In the privatization of the National Commercial Bank in Jamaica, for instance, the government provided information to the public in the areas of expected dividends and potential increase of prices in the future, and the result was in a successful sale.

(b) *Government credit:* In the case of lack of cash, the government should consider providing partial credit to buyers. This method has been widely adopted for buy-outs by employees. Government credit to private investors has, however, achieved mixed results. In the case of the Canadian Development Corporation with a value of Canadian $23 million, the first installment was paid on time. However, 1.8 million investors opted not to pay the additional amount required for the second installment when the share price had fallen from $11 to $6 a year later. In another case, the government of Canada was successful in the privatization of de Havilland Aircraft of Canada Ltd. to Boeing Co., which involved property values at Canadian $95 million in cash and $65 million in successive installments.

(c) *Assistance in obtaining banking credit:* Government can assist investors in obtaining banking credit through the provision of tax incentives to banks in respect of their loans for privatization purposes. In case of need for government loan guarantees, the government must act in a very prudent manner since it has no role in the firms' operation once they are privatized.

(d) *Attraction of foreign investment:* In order to attract foreign investors, government can take policy measures in such areas as tariffs, foreign exchange earnings, external trade regulations, and ownership.

(e) *Debt-equity swaps:* External debt is swapped for foreign direct or portfolio investment in a domestic firm, in either the private or the public sector. This measure originated in the 1980s in Argentina, Brazil, Chile, and Mexico, which had a high level of external debt. Subsequently, other countries, such as the Philippines and Jamaica, also adopted this device.

(f) *International technical assistance:* Governments of developing countries can and should request financial and technical support for their privatization from international development agencies. For instance, the United Nations Department for Development Support and Management Services provides technical support through advisory services, workshops, and publication of reports; the United Nations Development Programme provides financial assistance; the World Bank provides loans; and the Commonwealth Secretariat provides technical assistance to its members and some nonmember countries.

NOTES

1. World Bank, *World Development Report 1983,* published for the World Bank by Oxford University Press (1983). Countries discussed in the study were Argentina, the Dominican Republic, India, the Republic of Korea, Malawi, Panama, Sri Lanka, Tanzania, Tunisia, Turkey, and Zambia.

2. Major references for this section are as follows: Joseph Prokopenko and Igor Pavlin, ed., *Entrepreneurship Development in Public Enterprises,* Management Development Series No. 29 (Geneva, International Labour Office, 1991); United Nations, *Role and Extent of Competition in Improving the Performance of Public Enterprises,* TCD/SEM.89/2, INT-88-R59 (1989), Harvey Leibenstein and Dennis Roy, guest editors, *Entrepreneurship and Economic Development,* Journal of Development Planning, No. 18. United Nations publication Sales No. E.88.II.A.13 (1988).

3. For further discussion on this subject see Leibenstein and Roy, *Entrepreneurship and Economic Development,* pp. 21, 83, and 91.

4. For detailed discussions on this subject see Joseph J. Borgatti, "Method of Privatization of State-Owned Enterprises," paper prepared for a United Nations project, Transnational Corporations and Management Division, New York, May 1992.

5. For detailed discussions see D. M. Bhouraskar, "Financing Privatization: Role of Government," paper prepared for a United Nations project, Transnational Corporations and Management Division, New York, May 1992.

Chapter 9

ENTREPRENEURSHIP AND DEVELOPMENT OF SMALL AND MEDIUM ENTERPRISES

A. INTRODUCTION

It has been recognized that national entrepreneurship is essential to the promotion of economic development, employment, and technological advancement in both developed and developing countries.[1] In particular, the role of entrepreneurship in small and medium enterprises (SMEs) in promoting economic development has been widely recognized and documented.

There are many definitions of entrepreneurship given by various scholars. The essence of entrepreneurship includes a perception of innovation in response to changing environment and a willingness to interpret change as an opportunity for the creation of better performance. In the context of business operation, entrepreneurship includes two broad activities: creation of new products or services within existing enterprises and creation of new enterprises for new products or services.

In recent times, most countries have recognized the importance of entrepreneurship as an engine of economic growth and development. The extraordinary speed of economic development experienced by some countries, particularly in Asia, provides ample testimony to the now widely acknowledged fact that it is the conscious development of the entrepreneurial resources of nations and the role played by SMEs that determine their economic success. It is this widespread recognition of the importance of human resources in economic development that is responsible for the massive reform movement toward the ideology of free enterprise and market economy in Asia and other regions.

This is also evidenced by the recent development in both mixed and centrally planned economies, particularly in the East European countries and the former Soviet Union. These countries have begun to enhance entrepreneurship through the restructuring of their public enterprises. The strategies adopted vary among countries. As discussed in the preceding chapter, these include such measures as privatization, organizational reforms, and removal of institutional impediments to inspire entrepreneurship and to promote competition.

The objective of this chapter is to discuss some issues relating to entrepreneurship and SME development. The discussion treats the topics of promotion of entrepreneurship in labor-intensive SMEs, promotion of entrepreneurship in technology-intensive SMEs, policy environment and entrepreneurship development, and external support systems for entrepreneurship development. It will highlight selected country experience in Asia.

B. PROMOTING ENTREPRENEURSHIP IN LABOR-INTENSIVE SMEs

It has been a great concern of policymakers of developing countries to provide employment to the abundant supply of labor, given scarcity of capital, through the development of entrepreneurs and creation of enterprises. Two important issues are discussed here. One is market entry for the SMEs, especially in the service sector, which is fast becoming a lead sector in the economies of developing countries. The other is the promotion of subcontracting as a desirable way to develop SMEs.

B.1   Market Entry for SMEs Especially in the Service Sector

With growing prosperity in the economy, the service sector will become significantly important and even more so with the increasing trend of globalization of trade in services. The latter can be reflected by the available statistics, indicating that by the mid-1980s about 40 percent of the world stock in foreign direct investment and 50 percent of annual flows were in services, showing an increase of nearly 10 percentage points from the mid-1970s.[2] This implies that the service and manufacturing sectors will be the major source of employment creation for the vast pool of labor forces in the future.

Market entry by SMEs has been hindered by at least two barriers in many developing economies and in most centrally planned economies. One is the dominant position held by government-linked businesses in many services. SMEs have to compete against statutory boards of government enterprises that have enjoyed the privilege of government subsidies and easy access to government credit.

The other barrier to SME market entry is the increasing domination of key service industries by transnational corporations (TNCs). The increasing internationalization of services has been driven by a wide variety of forces, such as a growing demand for overseas services, internationalization of the advertising industry and services, and limited growth opportunities in the home market.

The preceding analysis indicates that existing as well as new SME service ventures will find themselves under increasing competitive pressure. This is not necessarily a threat to but an opportunity for SME service ventures since global economies and business integration create both expanding markets and multinational competition.

In turn, the analysis suggests that SMEs with limited resources will have to seek unique and varied ways of meeting competition. Among the major competitive advantages of SMEs are their entrepreneurship and innovation in terms of products, marketing, and business processes. There is not a standard form of innovation. Whereas U.S. firms have been most successful in making breakthroughs in product technology relating to technological innovation, Japanese firms tend to make incremental but continuous improvement in product design and process technology related to marketing innovation.

Related to the preceding is the marketing strategy of differentiation by SMEs. Differentiation includes creation of such components as new subtypes of old products, quality differentiation to satisfy potential customers for certain products, new delivery processes, new market segments of new locations, and extended hours of service.

B.2   Promoting Subcontracting as a Means for Developing SMEs

Subcontracting based on the principle of mutual benefit for SMEs and large corporations has been an effective method of promoting SMEs. Industrial policy should include provision for reserving certain items of production of spare parts and supplies and subassemblies in large enterprises exclusively for manufacture by SMEs.

Japan is a unique example of a country that has successfully instituted subcontracting through the combined efforts of the government, large parent corporations, and SME subcontractors. Through a variety of policy measures and institutional arrangements, SMEs play a key role as subcontractors for the machinery industry by making components for automobiles, electrical machine tools, and precision instruments in addition to the traditional production of daily commodities.

The successful Japanese experience has inspired other countries to adopt similar policy measures. For instance, in Korea, the subcontracting promotion law for small and medium industries originally legislated in 1975 was revised in 1978, and the government has employed a series of policy measures to enhance the subcontracting business. Under this revised law, the government designated some priority items for subcontracting, and the designated firms received preferential supports in the form of loans, easy access to foreign capital, and technical assistance. This enhanced the subcontracting system between primary firms producing assembly products and ancillary firms producing parts and components, thus improving the intraindustry division of labor. South Korea passed the Small and Medium Industry Systematization Promotion Law to ensure the development of an effective relationship for mutual advantage for both SMEs and large enterprises. Among others, the law contains provisions for settling any disputes re-

garding pricing of goods and delivery of products. As a result, SMEs increased
their role in industrialization by supplying more parts to the shipbuilding, auto-
mobile, and other machinery industries.

The policy measures that have been adopted by many countries cover a wide
variety of areas, including the following:

(a) Fiscal concessions and incentives to both contracting companies and
      subcontractors
(b) Purchase of a specific proportion of government procurements from SMEs
(c) Provision of subcontracting infrastructural facilities such as industrial
      parks
(d) Creation of support institutions
(e) Establishment of adequate technoeconomic information

C. PROMOTING ENTREPRENEURSHIP IN TECHNOLOGY-INTENSIVE SMEs

Technology-intensive SMEs have played a crucial role in a fast changing
globalized economy. Technology is considered necessary for stimulating innovations, creating new opportunities, helping diversification in both survival and
growth of existing enterprises, and ensuring a competitive advantage of SMEs
over large enterprises. Accordingly, there has been overwhelming concern regarding the development and absorption of new technology.

C.1 Exploitation of Niche Markets Through Innovations and Marketing

There is no established definition of niche market. Literally speaking, a niche
market can be defined as a new market that is created and developed by firms to
meet specific market situations through their competitive advantages. The experience in some Asian economies, in particular in Japan and Taiwan, indicates
that entrepreneurs in SMEs have been sensitive to the needs of customers and
have developed new products to exploit potential new niche markets based on
their adoption of high technologies and special marketing strategies. Adoption of
high technologies makes it possible to create new ventures and new businesses,
while adoption of innovative market strategy makes it possible to promote products in both new and old markets.

SMEs have been the driving force in niche markets; for instance in 1989,
there were nearly 6.6 million SME establishments in Japan, which accounted for
99 percent of all establishments. Similarly, SMEs accounted for 99 percent of all
establishments in Taiwan and 91 percent in the European community (with up to
10 employees). SMEs develop into small but strong global businesses through
their adoption of high technologies. One survey[3] indicates that more than 30

percent of small subcontracting manufacturers in Japan were at a technological levels either higher than or equal to that of their parent companies, representing an increase of 10 percentage points in comparison with the situation five years before. The survey also reveals that the percentage of SME subcontractors is only slightly lower than that of parent firms with respect to the introduction of factory automation in machinery-related industries. However, the percentage mentioned is substantially lower in SME subcontractors than in parent firms in the introduction of factory automation in computer-related industries.

It should be emphasized that niche marketing was a necessary but not a sufficient condition for market expansion. Technological innovation was crucial to market expansion. For instance, a government support program of Hsinchu Science-Based Industrial Park in Taiwan aims at promoting the transfer and development of technology, which in turn has resulted in stimulating a niche market for export promotion.

Successful niche marketing activities can be attributed to the following main factors:

(a)   Strong entrepreneurship spirit with a certain knowledge of technology and management
(b)   Ability and flexibility to adapt new technology and management to meet new circumstances
(c)   Innovative marketing strategies to meet changing market and consumer needs through such measures as product diversification and differentiation, with the primary motivation of generating new business and increasing profits

C.2   The Role of TNCs in Providing Technology and Marketing Know-How in SMEs

During the past decade, fear and resentment of transnational corporations (TNCs) have largely been replaced by recognition that TNCs can play a vital role in industrial and technological development mainly through their linkages with SMEs.

The Asian experience indicates two broad categories of linkages whereby SMEs can acquire modern technological know-how and receive market support for production activities from TNCs:

(a)   *Internal linkage:* This includes both ancillary operation and subcontracting. In ancillary operation SMEs do much of the production for domestic TNCs in the areas of machinery products and components and other engineering-related goods. Subcontracting denotes a contractual relationship in which SMEs supply TNCs specific and specialized products and services. Through this internal linkage TNCs support SMEs in terms of better access to national markets, know-how, raw materials, finance, and human resource development.

(b)   *External linkage:* Linkage between local SMEs and foreign TNCs involves various different forms and combinations. In the past, foreign TNCs primarily participated in Asian economies in the form of wholly foreign-owned TNC subsidiaries and offshore production and assembly units. Now they have gradually evolved into joint ventures and licensing contracts in order to make it easier to acquire foreign technology and to access foreign markets.

The business training of SME entrepreneurs must be viewed as an essential element of human resource development in the framework of TNC-SME linkages. Although entrepreneurship has been traditionally regarded as cultural heritage, education and training can also foster entrepreneurial talent. TNCs can build up SMEs' technological and managerial capacities through the participation of SMEs in all stages of design and engineering, turnover of experts and the secondment of staff to SMEs, and periodic conduct in training programs.

D.   POLICY ENVIRONMENT AND ENTREPRENEURSHIP DEVELOPMENT

Whereas SMEs are able to respond quickly and flexibly to market change and technological development through their close contact to customers, SMEs display structural disadvantages in comparison with large enterprises in such areas, with fewer opportunities to access financial sources, lower productivity due to less capital-intensive production equipment, and greater exposure to market failure caused by monopoly power, especially in the materials supply market. This suggests that there is a need for external supports in promoting SMEs.

In addition to cultural norms, government policies that foster supporting economic environment as well as directly supported entrepreneurial ventures are the basis for the development of entrepreneurship and the growth of national enterprise.

In Asia, macroeconomic policy has been moving within the framework of structural adjustment in a number of countries toward the greater use of SMEs in the economy.

D.1 Deregulation

Strong regulations build up powerful bureaucracies that, instead of playing a promotional role, often become an obstacle to SME development. Discrimination against private SMEs leads to the emergence of inefficiency and militates against internal and external competitiveness.

In the last two decades attitudes have been changing shifting away from discrimination against SMEs. In Japan, the overall macroeconomic policies at some stage of earlier development favored large industries. In Korea, "bigger is better" policies got hard lessons, in contrast to the successful experience of "small is beautiful" policies in Taiwan for promoting external trade. In both Japan and Korea, heavy industries could not be operated efficiently without local development of the parts and components industries. Therefore, SME policies and programs were introduced as measures to counteract the bias of favoring large enterprises. In Korea, a series of policy initiatives have been implemented since the late 1970s, including such measures as the requirement that commercial banks lend a certain proportion of annual incremental loans to SMEs (35 percent for nationwide banks and 80 percent for locally based banks) and the establishment of the Korea Credit Guarantee Fund in 1976, the Small and Medium Industry Promotion Fund, and its executive organization the Small and Medium Industry Promotion Corporation in 1978. In India, however, the favoring of SMEs was unrelated to government policy measures and was based on local cultural and political preferences.

The pace of the shift away from regulatory and discriminatory policies varied considerably from country to country according to national circumstances. However, in all cases the trend was toward more promotional and more flexible policies aimed at strengthening the competitiveness and technological dynamism of SMEs. Such measures include the following:

(a) Selected strategic SMEs were targeted for modernization and upgrading of equipment
(b) Financial and fiscal measures included special loan programs, investment credit, tax incentives, and privileged access to foreign exchange for promotion of SMEs
(c) Linkage between SMEs and TNCs such as subcontracting was strengthened. High-tech SMEs have an advantage over larger ones by acting faster in risk taking or adapting high technology and operating with more efficiency. However, large enterprises have stronger marketing organizations and more financial resources for commercialization than SMEs. Effective linkages of these two serve the interest of both groups
(d) Small enterprises were encouraged to merge and cooperate so as to obtain optimum plant size to prevent excessive competition and achieve greater operational efficiency.

D.2   Supportive Measures on Infrastructure and Human Resources

One important policy measure is the level of research and development (R & D) expenditure, which reflects the level of science and technology and national commitment in the development of technology-based industry. The United States commitment to R & D investment has been serving as a benchmark for technology development. But since 1985, Japan has been spending more on R & D investment as a percentage of its GNP than the United States. Available statistics indicate that this ratio was 2.9 percent for Japan in 1989 in comparison with 2.7 percent for the United States in 1990. In addition, nondefense expenditure as a proportion of total R & D expenditure is as high as 99 percent in Japan, compared to 70 percent in the United States. Among the newly industrializing economies, Korea has the highest ranking, with 1.92 percent of GNP on R & D expenditure in 1989, and Taiwan has the second highest ranking, with a ratio of 1.38 percent in 1989.

Government R & D spending plays an important role in technology ventures of SMEs that lack financial resources. In general, government R & D spending tends to be in basic research and high-risk areas, and its results remain in the public domain. That is, they are not geared toward commercial gains for any specific enterprise. The functions that government R & D spending performs in the growth of high-tech SMEs can be classified into the following broad categories:

(a)   Investment in higher education and public research institutes would accumulate human capital and serve as the breeding ground for entrepreneurs. In the case of the United States and Taiwan, for instance, college professors can accept consultancy to assist private industry, thus facilitating the linkage between the academic and commercial sectors. In the case of Japan, college professors are not permitted to accept research funds from commercial institutions, thus there is a lack of direct linkage between universities and the commercial sector in terms of technology development.

(b)   Government assistance in research organizations would facilitate the transfer of technology to SMEs. In Japan, small research institutes are established at the local government level and funded by local tax revenues. Their functions are to provide consulting services to SMEs and to facilitate the transfer of technology from other sectors. In Taiwan, a government funded agency of the Industrial Technology Research Institute aims at supporting the SMEs and is approaching the level of achievement in developed countries.

(c)   The purpose of government support of investment institutions is to finance direct investment in risky technology. In Japan, the Japan Key Technology Center was established in 1985 through the government's special account for industrial development. Their services include investment in R & D companies, conditional interest-free loans, facilitation of joint research, and R & D information services. Recently, Taiwan has adopted a similar approach by creating a government funded agency, the Industrial Technology Investment Corporation, which is an independent legal entity but is affiliated with the Industrial Technology Research Institute.

The other aspect of important government policy measures to support SMEs is the provision of infrastructure, including urban facilities to attract and retain high-tech engineers, communication services, and a system of laws and standards to conform with international practice.

The so-called industrial parks have been regarded as the most effective way to provide the right environment for advancing high-tech industries, particularly among SMEs. This subject is discussed further in Section D of Chapter 10.

Finally, technology is embodied not only in machines and equipment, as tangible assets, but also in people with technical and management skills, as intangible human assets. Human skills have been recognized as a major source of economic growth. In this regard, Taiwan and South Korea face a shortage of technological personnel that has recently been particularly serious in the case of SMEs. Although continuing emphasis should be placed on long-term aspects of science and technology education, each government has introduced policy measures to utilize the existing technological labor force effectively. The most common policy measure is preferential support for SMEs in the allocation of training and research facilities. In Korea, the government grants exemption from military duty for qualified young technicians and scientists who are employed in designated technology-intensive SMEs.

E. EXTERNAL COOPERATION ACTIVITIES

Given the existing and widening economic and technological gaps between developed and developing countries (as presented in Section B of Chapter 2 and Section B.2 of Chapter 10), there is a need for revitalizing technical cooperation among countries. External assistance to SMEs, including bilateral, regional, and international supports, has been important in complementing national programs through technical assistance, transfer of technology, and development of links among governments and institutions. Such assistance could take various forms, including expert advice, training programs, and provision of infrastructural facilities to strengthen entrepreneurial development in SMEs. The following are examples of external technical cooperation activities:

(a) Programs have been developed to strengthen the entrepreneurial spirit and to assist the creation of successful operation of new SMEs and expansion of existing ones. After a successful experience in Nepal, the German Technical Cooperation program embarked on a series of entrepreneurial development and training programs in Bangladesh, Sri Lanka, and the Philippines.

(b) A major constraint to SME development is the inability to find effective means for transfer of technology. Some donor agencies, including Canada, Germany, Scandinavian countries, and the United States, have developed technical cooperation programs on joint ventures for the transfer of technology and know-how to developing countries. Donor agencies provided facilities to SMEs of developing countries for easy access to markets, high-tech industries, and research institutes in donor countries.

(c)   In the last few years, United Nations agencies have provided target aid for creating new SMEs and entrepreneurial development to such special groups as women, disadvantaged ethnic minorities, refugees, and unemployed youth or graduates. In India, a special program for women has been developed to promote their participation as entrepreneurs in SME business, mainly in food-related industries and in the garment and craft industries, in a shift away from household and cottage enterprises.

In addition to the direct support through technical cooperation activities, the World Bank has implemented projects for financing SMEs since the 1970s, in view of the fact that its past loans for industrial development through development banks and other finance institutions did not benefit SMEs to any significant extent. To ensure effective implementation of credit programs for SMEs, lending by the World Bank is being done through commercial banks, which have a better financial network and more staff experienced in credit programs than development banks.

Similarly, the Asian Development Bank has provided financial assistance to SMEs within its region in the 1980s. The United States Agency for International Development has made loans and provided loan guarantees to SMEs in such countries as the Philippines and Thailand. The Netherlands Development Finance Company has given small credits through selected banks to SMEs in the Philippines, Thailand, and Sri Lanka.

These programs illustrate increased efforts made by donor agencies to provide financial credits to SMEs. Although the repayment of loans in some well-developed countries such as Korea were good, the rates were unsatisfactory in, for example, Bangladesh (less than 40 percent repayment), Nepal, and Indonesia (around 60 percent).

While emphasizing the need for strengthening technical assistance to developing countries from donor agencies, it is equally important to foster cooperation among the developing countries themselves. In Asia, Technonet Asia (headquartered in Singapore) and Asian Productivity Organization (headquartered in Japan) are examples of institutions to help establish and promote SMEs. Also, in the last few decades, several regional organizations for economic cooperation have been established, including the Association of South East Asian Nations, the Arab Common Market, and the Latin American Economic System. However, there continues to be a gap between achievements and intended objectives in the promotion of flow of trade, investment, and technology in these regional agencies. The point to be emphasized here is that the existing regional cooperation agencies can facilitate certain institutional arrangements for SME promotion. Such arrangements could include activities relating to the coordination of various SME promotion programs within the region, exchange of information and experience, and creation of a focal point for receiving external assistance. In this regard, the North America Free Trade Agreement drafted in August 1992 for the United States, Canada, and Mexico and the framework of the single market of the European Economic Community proposed in 1992 could provide useful experience to other regions of developing countries in terms of cooperation on trade, investment, and SME development.

Finally, external technical cooperation assistance has yielded some valuable lessons. For instance, to have an effective and significant impact on recipient countries, programs of assistance should meet the specific needs of the country. In addition, donor agencies should not impose the experience of other countries when it is unrealistic for the country concerned in the light of its specific conditions.

Another lesson relates to the relative effectiveness of project implementation through nongovernment organizations versus government agencies. Nongovernment organizations appear to have more grass-root impact through their voluntary groups, social and religious agencies, and self-help organizations than government agencies. One good example is the World Assembly of Small and Medium Enterprises, which is noted for its support of SMEs. In addition to nongovernmental organizations, project implementation by private sector organizations using external donor funds has the advantage of less bureaucracy and closer contact with the target groups over government counterpart organizations.

NOTES

1. Major references for this chapter are the background papers of the Symposium on Entrepreneurship and Economic Development in Asia, New Delhi, India, 22-25 October 1991, organized jointly by the United Nations and the World Assembly of Small and Medium Enterprises.

2. United Nations, *Transnational Corporations in World Development – Trends and Prospects,* United Nations publication Sales No. E.88.II.A.7 (1988), pp. 4-6, 84-87.

3. Small and Medium Enterprise Agency, Ministry of International Trade and Industry, *Small Business in Japan 1991: White Paper on Small and Medium Enterprise in Japan* (1991).

Chapter 10

EFFECTIVE TRANSFER AND DEVELOPMENT OF TECHNOLOGY

A. INTRODUCTION

Acquiring the most advanced technology may be a necessary but not a sufficient condition for ensuring its mastery, adaptation, and development.[1] Effective transfer and utilization of technology imports require a strategy that the recipient country must develop domestically a holistic approach in the areas of identifying and designing a specific need for technology, developing human resources, and setting up an efficient institutional and economic policy framework. Most principles and frameworks for effective transfer and development of technology in the context of technical assistance through bilateral or multilateral cooperation as presented in this chapter are equally applicable to commercial transfer of technology.

There is a widespread recognition that scientific and technological advances have an increasingly decisive influence on the achievement of sustained economic growth and development.[2] The application of environmentally sound technologies can contribute significantly to raising production both qualitatively and quantitatively and is associated with changes in income and employment. Also, technologies can contribute to conservation and sustainability of natural resources in such areas as agricultural production, renewable energy generation, and pollution control, which are the prevailing concerns regarding sustainable development of the world.

The transfer of technology is as important as the development of technology in promoting economic development. The transfer of technology is particularly important in achieving sustainable development in a situation where a country lacks its own capacity for developing technology domestically. Here are some examples:

(a)   Two hundred years ago, imports of machinery and emigration of skilled labor from Europe helped the United States build a new world.

(b)   After the Second World War, Japan was highly successful at introducing
       established technology from more advanced countries.
(c)   In the last two to three decades, adaptation of appropriate technologies
       from industrialized countries together with promotion of foreign trade
       provided the engine for accelerating economic growth in several devel-
       oping countries. This is particularly evidenced by the four more advanced
       developing economies of Hong Kong, the Republic of Korea, Singapore,
       and Taiwan.

Most technologies needed by developing countries for improving their productive capacity and accelerating their technological transformation are available in developed countries. For instance, there still exists a great potential for
transferring existing old technologies from developed to developing countries in
the areas of fertilizer, food processing, and electronic products. In this regard, a
major challenge for the world community in the 1990s and beyond is how to
elaborate and implement a strategy of transferring technologies from industrialized countries and applying them in a manner that is compatible with developing
economies. A large part of this challenge will be to assure the widest possible
diffusion of the technologies, overcoming such obstacles as export restrictions by
developed countries and ability to pay for them. Also, there is a need for further
trade liberalization by developed countries to permit the export of high technologies to developing countries for fostering the technological transformation of those
that have financial capabilities to do so.

One important aspect of international technical assistance through bilateral or
multilateral cooperation is promotion of transfer and development of technology.
Though the volume of technology transfer through international technical assistance is relatively small in comparison with that of commercial transactions
through trade and investment, it does reflect profoundly the spirit and willingness of the international community in promoting exchanges on science and technology.

The following presents a brief review of trends of transfer of technology. This
is followed by a discussion on factors affecting effective transfer and development
of technology. A remark on industrial parks is given in the last section.

B.   A BRIEF REVIEW OF TRENDS IN TRANSFER OF TECHNOLOGY

The term *transfer of technology* is often subject to different interpretations.
Technology is the technical and management knowledge or know-how that leads
to the production of improved machinery, products, and services. Advance in this
knowledge through research reduces the real cost of producing the existing products and services and leads to the introduction of new products and services with
improved quality. The word *technology* itself comprises at least the following
categories:

(a)   Tangible assets of capital goods, such as tools, machinery, equipment and entire production systems
(b)   Intangible assets, such as methods and techniques, design, project feasibility study and blueprints
(c)   Human skills such as management and organizational structure

In line with the preceding discussion, the meaning of *transfer of knowledge* includes not only the physical transfer of advanced technical means, but also the development of human skills to adapt them effectively and the cultivation of innovation capability to develop new products and services.[3] The process of acquiring technological capacity from abroad requires three distinct but interrelated stages:

(a)   The transfer and utilization of existing technologies to produce specific goods and services
(b)   The assimilation, absorption, adaptation, and diffusion of these technologies to the host economy
(c)   The further development and simulation of indigenous capacities for innovation

The need for strengthening transfers of technology is inspired in part by the vast changes in the international economic and political environment during the last decade or so. In particular, these new global developments are the Uruguay Round negotiations for a new trade agreement, the negotiation on an International Code of Conduct on the Transfer of Technology, the opening up of opportunities in China and Eastern Europe and the USSR for free flow of investments and trade, and trade liberalization policies pursued by many countries.

The renewed concern about transfer of technology includes at least the following three issues: (1) the decreasing trend in the transfer of technology, (2) the widening gap of technology between developed and developing countries, and (3) the strengthening of mechanisms for achieving broader technical cooperation on transfer of technology among countries.

B.1   Decreasing Trend in the Transfer of Technology

In contrast to its rapid expansion in 1960s and 1970s,[4] the international flow of technology, particularly to developing countries as a group, had shown stagnation or even decline during the first half of the 1980s.[5] Table 10.1 presents indicators of international technology flow (1980-1988). Although not displaying a consistent pattern of declining trend, this table indicates that capital goods export from the developed market economy countries (DMECs) to the developing countries (DCs) showed a decrease from US$114.3 billion in 1980 to US$102.8 billion in 1984. Similarly, foreign direct investment flows from the world to DCs re-

Table 10.1
Indicators of International Technology Flows (1980–1988) (billions of dollars, current prices)

Indicator	1980	1981	1982	1983	1984	1985	1986	1987	1988	Growth 1980/81 to 1987/88	Growth 1984/85 to 1987/88
A. Capital goods exports[a]											
1. DMECs to world	356.4	365.7	350.6	340.3	367.6	389.2	469.1	557.4	628.7	7.3	25.2
2. DMECs to DMECs	216.1	213.7	206.1	212.0	241.0	261.4	326.3	399.5	452.9	10.2	30.2
3. DMECs to DCs	114.3	127.9	120.6	104.4	102.8	97.8	107.7	126.2	143.5	1.5	16.0
4. DMECs to Eastern Europe	11.1	9.5	9.9	10.5	8.6	9.0	11.8	11.7	13.3	2.8	19.2
5. Eastern Europe to DCs	6.9	7.1	7.5	7.2	8.7	6.6	---	---	---	---	---
6. DCs to DMECs	13.6	15.5	17.0	21.3	28.1	28.4	33.9	44.7	56.3	21.7	49.2
7. DCs to DCs	12.0	14.0	13.2	12.7	13.3	12.9	11.2	12.4	---	-1.6	---
B. Foreign direct investment flows											
8. World to DMECs	41.3	42.6	30.0	33.5	38.6	35.7	63.6	94.5	118.8	14.2	69.4
9. World to DCs	10.8	14.9	13.9	9.8	10.9	11.7	12.1	21.4	22.3	7.9	39.2
10. DCs to world	1.1	0.2	1.1	0.8	0.4	0.6	0.8	1.7	5.0	26.4	160.8
C. Technology payments											
11. World to DMECs	16.7	20.7	21.2	23.6	24.2	24.9	38.0	42.6	47.8	28.0	35.6
12. DCs to DMECs[b]	2.2	2.4	2.2	2.5	2.4	1.4	---	---	---	---	---
D. Technical co-operation grants											
13. DMECs to DCs	7.3	7.4	7.4	7.7	7.7	8.2	9.6	11.6	12.6	7.4	23.0

Memo item:	1980	1981	1982	1983	1984	1985	1986	1987	1988
Export unit values of manufacturers exported by DMECs (1980 = 100)	100	95	92	89	86	87	103	112	124

Source: UNCTAD secretariat computations based on data from (i) United Nations, for capital goods exports; (ii) UNCTC, for foreign direct investment flows; (iii) OECD STIID Data Bank for technology payments from world to DMECs, national sources from OECD countries for royalties and fees (indicator 12); and (iv) OECD for technical co-operation grants. *Table source*: United Nations, *Transfer and Development of Technology in a Changing World Environment: The Challenges of the 1990s*, United Nations publication, Sales No. TD/C.6/156 (1991), p. 3.

[a] Includes SITC/Rev. 1, Section 7, Machinery and Transport equipment except 7194 domestic appliances, non-electrical; 7241 television receivers; 7242 radio broadcast receivers; 7250 domestic electric equipment; 7321 passenger motor cars; 7326 chassis for passenger motor cars; 7329 motor cycles; and 7331 bicycles.

[b] Flows into France, Federal Republic of Germany, Japan, Italy, and United States only.

(---) = not available.

mained almost unchanged statistically with US$10.9 billion in 1984 in compari-son with US$10.8 billion in 1980. When the preceding statistics expressed in current prices are converted into real terms, they reflect a deeper decline in the transfer of technology to the developing world.

This trend had been in part due to sluggish growth in the world economy and its depressing effect on export earnings by developing countries. Other contribut-ing factors of this declining trend include the debt crisis, the decline in the prices of export commodities, protectionism in industrialized countries, and the replace-ment of raw materials by new materials produced through technological innova-tion. Another important factor, which is not explicitly addressed in the statistical report, is the "brain drain," which has caused a reverse flow of technological human resources from developing to developed countries.

The period between 1985 and 1988 brought changes in the increase of growth, direction, and composition of international technology flows. Foreign direct in-vestment to developing countries grew faster than merchandise trade of capital goods exports, thus pointing to the growing importance of the transfer of technol-ogy in shaping the global network of economic relationships.

Within the developing world, there exists a wide disparity on trends in tech-nology flows among regions and countries (see Table 10.2). By geographical re-gion, flows of foreign direct investment to developing Asia surged even more rapidly than to other regions between 1985 and 1988. As a proportion of technol-ogy-related inflows of capital goods, foreign direct investment and technical co-operation grants to developing countries climbed up to 56 percent in 1988 to developing Asia. It was the first time in history that developing Asia had over-taken Latin America as the major recipient of foreign direct investment among developing countries. By analytical group, major exporters of manufactures, in-cluding Brazil, Hong Kong, Mexico, the Republic of Korea, Singapore, Taiwan, and Yugoslavia, accounted for 35 percent of technology-related inflows to devel-oping countries in 1988.

B.2 Widening Technology Gap Between Developed and Developing Countries

A dichotomous analysis of technological development often divides the world into two parts: Developed countries innovate and export new technologies, while developing countries imitate and supply imitated goods. The two activities are taking place continuously and there continues to exist a persistent technology gap between the developed and developing countries.

Of the recent acceleration of technological advances, the areas of biotechnol-ogy, materials, and microelectronics appear to create a more complex competitive environment that will have far-reaching effects on technology diffusion in the 1990s and beyond. The existing country differences in industrial, scientific, and technological base and investment capabilities would suggest the strong possibil-

Table 10.2
Technology-Related Flows to and from Developing Countries and Territories (billions of dollars)

Indicator	All Developing countries[a]		By geographical region						By analytical group				China[c]	
			Developing America		Developing Africa		Developing Asia		Major exporters of manufacturers[b]		Least developed countries[b]			
	Inflow	Outflow	Inflow	Outflow	Inflow	Outflow	Inflow	Outflow	Inflow	Outflow	Inflow	Outflow	Inflow	Outflow
I. Capital goods[d]														
1980	114	14	32	4	25	-	54	9	24	8	4	-	4	-
1981	128	16	36	4	27	1	62	10	24	9	3	-	3	-
1982	121	17	29	5	23	-	66	12	21	10	3	-	2	-
1983	104	21	21	5	19	-	63	15	20	13	3	-	3	-
1984	103	28	24	7	18	-	58	20	23	17	3	-	4	-
1985	98	28	26	8	17	-	53	20	23	18	3	-	10	-
1986	108	34	29	9	17	1	58	24	29	22	3	-	11	-
1987	126	45	32	10	16	1	74	32	46	30	4	-	9	1
1988	144	56	36	13	17	1	87	41	56	39	4	-	9	1
II. Foreign direct investment														
1980	10.8	1.1	7.1	0.4	0.3	0.1	3.2	0.6	4.4	0.4	0.3	-	-	0
1981	14.9	0.2	7.6	0.2	1.5	0.1	5.6	0.1	6.3	0.2	0.3	-	0.3	0
1982	13.9	1.1	7.4	0.4	1.4	0.1	4.9	0.6	5.5	0.8	0.2	-	0.4	-
1983	9.8	0.8	4.0	0.3	1.2	0.1	4.4	0.4	3.6	0.4	-	-	0.6	0.1
1984	10.9	0.4	4.7	0.1	1.4	0.1	4.7	0.3	4.0	0.2	0.1	-	1.3	0.1
1985	11.7	0.6	5.6	0.1	2.6	-	3.4	0.4	3.5	0.4	0.1	-	1.7	0.6
1986	12.1	0.8	6.1	0.2	1.8	-	4.2	0.6	2.8	0.5	-	-	1.9	0.4
1987	21.4	1.7	10.8	0.2	2.2	0.1	8.2	1.4	6.5	1.3	0.2	-	2.3	0.6
1988	22.3	5.0	9.3	0.1	2.8	-	9.9	4.8	7.0	4.5	0.2	-	3.2	0.8

154

Indicator	All Developing countries[a]		By geographical region						By analytical group				China[c]	
			Developing America		Developing Africa		Developing Asia		Major exporters of manufacturers[b]		Least developed countries[b]			
	Inflow	Outflow	Inflow	Outflow	Inflow	Outflow	Inflow	Outflow	Inflow	Outflow	Inflow	Outflow	Inflow	Outflow
III. Technical co-operation grants[e]														
1980	7.3		1.2		3.1		1.8		0.2		1.5		0.1	
1981	7.4		1.2		3.0		1.8		0.2		1.6		0.1	
1982	7.4		1.0		3.0		1.9		0.2		1.6		0.1	
1983	7.7		1.0		3.2		1.8		0.2		1.6		0.1	
1984	7.7		1.2		3.2		1.7		0.2		1.6		0.1	
1985	8.2		1.2		3.5		1.8		0.2		1.8		0.1	
1986	9.6		1.5		4.1		2.1		0.3		2.1		0.2	
1987	11.5		1.8		4.7		2.5		0.3		2.4		0.3	
1988	12.6		2.0		4.9		2.9		0.4		2.6		0.3	

Source: UNCTAD secretariat computations based on data from: (i) United Nations, for capital goods imports; (ii) UNCTC, for foreign direct investment; and (iii) OECD, for technical co-operation grants. Table source: United Nations, *Transfer and Development of Technology in a Changing World Environment: The Challenges of 1990s*, United Nations publication, Sales No. TD/C.6/156 (1991), p.4.

a Total also includes developing countries and territories of Europe and Oceania, and is subject to rounding.
b Major exporters of manufacturers: Brazil, Hong Kong, Mexico, Republic of Korea, Singapore, Taiwan Province of China and Yugoslavia. Least developed countries: See UNCTAD, *Handbook of international trade and development statistics, 1989*, United Nations Sales No. E/F.90.II.D.I., September 1990.
c Memo item.
d See *footnote* a in table I for definition.
e Grants that the donors have not allocated to individual countries are not included in the regional or analytical groups, but are included in the total for developing countries.

ity that the recent technological advances will continue to widen the industrial and technological polarization between developed and developing countries and among developing countries as well. The developed countries are endowed with these comparative advantages to lead the development of these high technologies, which require very high-tech innovations and involve increasing costs of research and development. Parallel to this development is the trend toward strengthening intellectual property rights protection by developed countries, thus protecting innovations from imitation by developing countries.

The diffusion of these advanced technologies will present a challenge to developing countries in the 1990s. There is no systematic empirical evidence to suggest that the overall impact of advanced technologies on competitiveness and technology transfer in the developing countries will be adverse. However, there is a strong possibility that those developing countries with inadequate education and skills levels coupled with crippling financial constraints will find themselves inadequate for diffusion of more advanced technologies and for attraction of foreign investment in new plant and equipment based on these advanced technologies. Also, some have expressed concern that the spread of these advanced technologies, in particular electronic automation and new materials, may cause developing countries to lose their attractiveness as low-labor-cost locations for production.

Contrasts in technological development and related economic performance also exist among developing countries (see Table 10.3). For instance, in terms of the levels of industrialization, the four more industrially advanced developing economies of East Asia have the highest shares of manufacturing in GDP, in ascending order, Singapore, Hong Kong, the Republic of Korea, and Taiwan, ranging from 27 to 43 percent in 1987. In terms of accumulated external patents granted in the United States from 1962 to 1987, the four highest economies are, in ascending order, Brazil, Argentina, Taiwan, and Mexico in the range from 478 to 1301. These statistics are substantially higher than those of least developing countries.

B.3   The Strengthening of Technical Cooperation

The stagnation of technology flows to developing countries and the widening technology gap between developed and developing countries as presented in the preceding analysis would suggest the need for revitalizing technical cooperation among all countries. It appears from Table 10.1 that the growth rate of technical cooperation grants in noncommercial form from developed market economy countries to developing countries was as high as 23 percent from 1984/85 to 1987/88, in contrast with 7.4 percent from 1980/81 to 1987/88. However, this noncommercial form of technical cooperation grants in absolute terms has been relatively small in comparison with commercial technology flows. Nevertheless, the former channel for the transfer of technology was reported to have been of particular

Table 10.3
Technological Development and Related Economic Performance

29 developing countries and territories by region	Manufacturing value added		MVA[a] In capital goods Industry[b]			Capital stock per employee in manufacturing[c]			Productivity[d]		ICOR[e]		World market share in manufactured exports			External patenting[f] accumulated 1962-1987	
	Growth	as % of GDP	Growth		as % of GDP	Growth		Value	Growth				% change		%	No.[g]	No.[h]
	1970-1987	1987	1970-1980	1980-1987	1987	1972-1980	1980-1988	1988	1970-1980	1980-1987	1970-1979	1980-1988	1970-1980	1980-1988	1988		
Côte d'Ivoure	3.3	9	1.3	2.0	2.1	2	-3	4	-0.4	1.3	3.3	17.2	-0.002	0.006	0.013	4	0.49
Egypt	6.2	11	-0.8	4.2	1.3	11	4	1	2.3	3.3	2.8	2.7	-0.045	0.060	0.076	35	0.84
Kenya	7.6	12	-1.3	-5.6	0.7	6	-1	1	2.1	1.3	5.6	6.2	-0.004	-0.003	0.005	23	1.37
Nigeria	5.2	4	21.0	-17.2	0.7	16	-1	2	0.0	-0.8	5.1	:	-0.013	-0.004	0.003	22	0.27
Tunisia	9.7	14	11.9	4.3	1.8	8	3	3	3.3	2.0	4.2	9.1	0.024	0.011	0.048	13	2.03
United Rep. of Tanzania	0.5	7	6.7	-12.0	0.4	3	-9	1	-3.7	-3.8	6.5	15.1	-0.002	-0.001	0.002	9	0.48
Zambia	1.6	20	5.7	1.7	3.0	:	:	5	-2.0	0.6	44.0	44.0	-0.076	-0.019	0.037	11	1.95
Argentina	0.5	24	-1.3	1.9	7.0	6	-1	30	3.1	2.5	9.0	:	0.017	-0.007	0.083	520	18.71
Brazil	5.7	25	1.8	-0.4	5.7	6	-1	13	1.0	1.3	3.2	7.1	0.250	0.134	0.486	4	3.94
Chile	1.0	21	-6.5	-2.8	1.5	0	-1	7	2.8	2.4	13.4	11.9	-0.021	-0.021	0.109	79	7.10
Colombia	4.6	22	2.3	-1.9	2.0	3	4	6	1.8	4.2	3.1	6.0	0.017	-0.007	0.029	110	4.26
Costa Rica	5.1	19	5.2	-3.1	1.2	:	:	:			3.8	11.9	0.004	-0.007	0.008	32	14.04
Ecuador	5.8	17	8.0	-1.1	1.4	8	2	4	0.5	1.9	:	:	0.003	-0.002	0.001	33	4.06
Guatemala	3.1	16	-0.1	-5.7	0.5	4	-6	1	1.9	0.1	3.3	23.1	-0.003	-0.017	0.003	45	6.51
Mexico	4.3	21	1.9	-3.2	2.9	3	3	7	3.6	2.3	3.5	:	-0.041	0.147	0.252	1301	18.75
Peru	3.0	21	6.5	-9.0	1.7	3	-2	5	0.1	2.9	6.9	:	-0.006	-0.035	0.037	67	3.87
Uruguay	1.5	22	0.4	-0.1	2.8	0	2	4	3.4	5.5	3.8	:	0.003	-0.002	0.016	:	:
Venezuela	4.1	19	9.2	-0.3	2.2	4	3	11	-2.7	3.6	6.0	41.2	0.018	-0.007	0.027	220	14.64

Table 10.3
Technological Development and Related Economic Performance (Continued)

29 developing countries and territories by region	Manufacturing value added		MVA[a] in capital goods industry[b]			Capital stock per employee in manufacturing[c]			Productivity[d]		ICOR[e]		World market share in manufactured exports			External patenting[f] accumulated 1962-1987	
	Growth	as % of GDP	Growth		as % of GDP	Growth		Value	Growth				% change		%	No.[g]	No.[h]
	1970-1987	1987	1970-1980	1980-1987	1987	1972-1980	1980-1988	1988	1970-1980	1980-1987	1970-1979	1980-1988	1970-1980	1980-1988	1988		
Hong Kong	13.4	30	..	..	6.1	..	9	3	0.1	6.7	3.8	4.2	0.590	0.650	1.640	387	76.81
India	5.7	19	1.3	3.2	2.9	3	4	2	7.4	7.6	7.4	3.9	-0.071	0.015	0.237	301	0.44
Indonesia	11.8	17	22.0	7.4	1.1	18	10	4	0.9	-0.5	2.1	6.4	0.041	0.136	0.183	75	0.50
Malaysia	9.9	24	13.8	1.3	3.5	7	1	4	5.0	6.5	3.1	8.0	-0.002	0.070	0.232	74	5.38
Pakistan	6.9	17	2.6	-0.2	0.9	-4	9	2	-2.6	8.2	3.4	4.0	-0.055	0.024	0.080	15	0.17
Philippines	3.8	24	0.9	-10.8	0.8	15	1	1	5.8	5.6	3.5	54.6	0.077	0.031	0.133	132	2.73
Rep. of Korea	13.6	34	9.7	8.7	10.3	15	11	15	1.7	6.9	2.7	4.0	0.543	0.703	1.412	331	8.68
Singapore	8.1	27	8.7	1.9	16.9	11	8	18	11.9	6.5	4.8	8.5	0.362	0.331	0.813	76	31.48
Taiwan Prov. of China	11.2	43	..	..	10.3	..	..	..	3.4	7.7	3.9	4.1	0.497	1.080	1.630	1289	72.40
Thailand	8.4	22	6.1	0.6	3.0	3	8	4	0.9	8.1	3.6	4.7	0.067	0.124	0.236	19	0.41
Turkey	6.7	27	5.6	1.2	2.7	7	6	11		5.7	4.3	3.1	0.020	0.170	0.206	41	0.92

Source: UNCTAD secretariat computations based on data from UNSO, UNIDO, IMF, OECD, and United States Patent Office. Table source: United Nations, *Transfer and Development of Technology in a Changing World Environment: The Challenge of the 1990s*, United Nations publication, Sales No. TD/C.6/156 (1991), p. 18.

a Manufacturing value added.
b Capital goods industry defined as output of ISIC 381 to ISIC 385.
c For the computation of capital stock, see notes to figure 1. The values in 1988 are relative values only. They are estimated on the assumption that the share of capital goods in the manufacturing sector is proportional to the share of the manufacturing sector in total GDP.
d Value added per employee in the manufacturing sector.
e Incremental capital output ratio (ICOR) for the period i to j is defined as the ratio of gross fixed investment over the period i minus 1 to j minus 1 to output in period j minus output in period i.
f External patents granted in the United States, accumulated 1962 to 1987.
g Accumulated patents 1962 to 1987.
h Per million population (1980).

significance in the accumulation of the skills and know-how that have buttressed the growth of exports of certain South East Asian economies.

Several international actions can be envisaged for encouraging technology transfer to developing countries. The following illustrates several potential avenues:

(a) There is a need to strengthen noncommercial forms of technical grants to developing countries. This includes provision of technical experts for assisting project design in technology development and training of engineers, technicians, and research and development personnel.

(b) Restoring technology flows to developing countries would be difficult unless the global economic environment were improved in order to revive and sustain the growth and development of developing countries. Decisive steps must be taken by the international community to solve the debt and balance-of-payments problems of developing countries.

(c) Developed countries could consider such policy measures as concessional credit for technology transfer and tax incentives, that is, greater possibilities for offsetting losses on foreign investments against home-country tax liabilities.

(d) The international trade and investment issues such as the International Code of Conduct on Transfer of Technology and protection of intellectual property must take full account of the developmental, trade, and technological objectives of developing countries.

While emphasizing the need for strengthening technical cooperation between developed and developing countries, there is also a necessity to foster cooperation among developing countries. Developing countries constitute a heterogenous group and differ widely in terms of size, levels of socioeconomic development, endowments of natural resources, technological capacity, and trade and financial constraints. Taken together, developing countries are endowed with considerable natural, human, and financial resources. They could enjoy complementarities by adapting and generating technologies suitable to their common needs.

The kinds of schemes on technological linkages among developing countries could draw on the experience of the North America Free Trade Agreement of Canada, Mexico, and the United States proposed in August 1992, and the proposed single market framework of the European Economic Community in 1992. The removal of trade and investment barriers between countries and the advantage of economies of scale in a larger market will foster the transfer and development of technology among countries.

Several regional organizations for economic cooperation have been established in developing countries in the last few decades. These include the regional schemes such as the Association of South East Asian Nations (ASEAN), the Arab Common Market, the Latin American Economic System, the Caribbean Community and Common Market, and the Latin American Free Trade Association. Although flows of trade, investment, and technology among developing countries of each region are increasing, a gap between objectives and achievements continues.[6]

Experience with different kinds of efforts undertaken by the various regional schemes indicates that many policy measures and legal statutes are not realistic or adequate to achieve the intended goals. To strengthen mechanisms for achieving broader technical cooperation, consideration should be given to more adequate and specific instruments in areas such as avoidance of double taxation, patent legislation, harmonization of "buy regional" goods and services schemes, information systems, brokerage centers, and direct financial and technical assistance to be furnished by special agencies created within or under the umbrella of regional organizations.

C. FACTORS AFFECTING EFFECTIVE TRANSFER AND DEVELOPMENT OF TECHNOLOGY

One criticism of foreign technology transfer to developing countries is the failure to realize the difficulties and constraints that are so often faced by many developing countries in their quest to acquire foreign technology. In many cases, the technical cooperation programs are ill designed by donor/export agencies in that they do not really respond to particular priorities of recipient countries. The recipient country often lacks supporting economic and technical environment and political will to lay a good foundation for successful implementation.

Careful assessments must be made to define the technological requirements associated with the development strategy of the economy. Experience has been gained in some developing economies with varying degrees of success in adaptation and recreation of appropriate technologies in the context of their socioeconomic environment. The four more industrially advanced developing economies of East Asia display a wide range of strategies and a vast array of industrial structures. Hong Kong is the closest to the neoliberal paradigm of free trade. Comparatively speaking, its industrial structure involves a high reliance on foreign technology with a good proportion of light consumer goods for export. By contrast, the Republic of Korea has come closest to emulating the Japanese strategy. It emphasizes a high degree of government selective intervention, especially in heavy and high-technology activities. It has built a diversified industrial base with a high degree of local integration and well-developed local design and innovation capabilities. Taiwan is closer to the Republic of Korea in that it has developed local technologies and chosen selective intervention and an often high degree of protection, even though it has been less interventionist in promoting heavy industry in the past. Promotion of high technology began in the late 1980s and will continue in the 1990s. Singapore has entered into heavy industry through its intervention in the direction of investment flows rather than via protection. Technology is mostly provided from abroad with little local innovation.

Each country must adopt its own specific strategy in accordance with its unique technical and economic requirements. However, there exists a common framework for successful transfer and development of technology.[7] In the present discussion, particular emphasis is placed on the following three points: (1) appropriate technology and absorptive capacity, (2) human resources development and entrepreneurship, and (3) government policies and measures.

C.1 Appropriate Technology and Absorptive Capacity

There is an obvious relationship between the level of development of the recipient country and the options of technology open to it. Factors affecting the form of technology transfer embrace not merely financial resources, but most importantly the technological requirements associated with development. Also careful assessments must be made not only to ensure technological coherence but also to exploit complementarities among various elements of the productive sectors as well as between the technologically modern and backward segments of society.

In designing a macroeconomic framework for effective transfer and development of appropriate technology, one should consider the following three factors: (1) diffusion of technology throughout the whole economy, (2) stimulation of local technological activities and participation by small and medium enterprises, and (3) absorptive capacities.

(1)   *Diffusion of technology throughout the economy:* Most important of all, there is a need for a clear articulation of a development strategy, to which the strategy of technology importation can be closely related. The Japanese experience has become a "model" that has in many ways inspired the technology policies of some developing countries with various degrees of success in transfer and development of technology.[8] Soon after the end of the Second World War, Japanese planners systematically pursued a capital-and-technology-intensive strategy based on heavy industry, deliberately eschewing labor-intensive and light industry as its industrialization path. The Ministry of International Trade and Industry (MITI) and the Foreign Investment Council coordinated a "staggered entry" of new technology. Large industrial enterprises were guaranteed a certain domestic market share during the "learn by doing" period when new capital-intensive and high technologies were imported. This also enabled recipient firms to assimilate and adapt imported technology and eventually to develop innovative capacity. By the 1970s, although Japan was still a major technology importer, it had already started to export technology, principally to developing countries at first, and then increasingly to other developed countries.

One important objective of acquiring foreign technologies is to have a strong influence on the macroeconomic environment. It must take into account local economic conditions such as factor prices, input availability, and market characteristics. For instance, many developing countries have specific geographical and socioeconomic conditions, such as dryland farming and small-scale enterprises. In this particular situation, the existing commercial suppliers of technology from abroad cannot readily meet the local conditions and therefore need to modify them to suit local needs. Necessary steps must also be taken to prevent adverse environmental effects of pollution and exploitation of natural resources.

One should also weigh carefully a trade-off between short- and long-term costs and returns when deciding among alternative forms of technology transfers. Comparatively speaking, direct investments are mostly managed by foreign partners with expert staffs and yield a stream of outputs in a shorter period. In contrast, import of technology in an unpackaged form places greater responsibilities on local firms and is likely to have higher short-term costs in the form of delays, errors, and cost overruns. However, the externalities of unpackaging are greater than those of foreign direct investment in the long run in that experience gained from the former could lead to substantial technological benefits and to a reduction in costs.

(2)   *Stimulation of local technological activities and participation by small and medium enterprises:* There are a number of ways that technical cooperation can stimulate local technological activities. For instance, local engineers in recipient countries participate in all stages of design and engineering; the parent corporations turn over experts and second staff to local firms; and local firms conduct joint research with parent corporations on adaptations of the product to special local market conditions.

The extent to which new technologies can stimulate local development depends on the types of technologies and forms of technical cooperation.[9] In the case of assembly procedures for the technologically most sophisticated semiconductors, for example, the research, design, and production are mostly undertaken in the headquarters of parent corporations in the developed countries. Only the assembly and test operations are undertaken in the recipient countries for reexport, thus giving limited linkage effects to the local technology of development. In the case of joint venture arrangements the partners in both exporting and recipient countries share jointly the control and benefits. Thus the nature and quality of technology transfer tend to be more explicit.

In promoting the transfer and development of technology, small and medium enterprises (SMEs) in both developed and developing countries have played an indispensable role. Many studies have concluded that SMEs account for a great proportion of entrepreneurial talents and technological innovations although their R & D expenditure is comparatively small. They are major agents in the adaptation, propagation, and dissemination of the results of applied research and technical innovations. One study in the Republic of Korea found that SMEs with fewer than 100 workers accounted for 63 percent of the innovative machineries as designated by the government.[10]

SMEs in exporting countries have also played an important role in export activities and technology transfer, although their local market share has been relatively modest. In Japan as early as the 1950s, SMEs contributed about 70 percent of Japanese exports, whereas in France (1978) and Italy (1981) firms with fewer than 500 employees accounted for 29 percent and 47 percent, respectively, of the total exports of goods and services. Similarly, a survey of firms in the northeast part of the United Kingdom (1971) revealed that 62 percent of the exporters were SMEs.[11]

In a study on the experience of Western European SMEs in the transfer of technology through joint ventures and technology arrangements in Latin America, the evidence indicates that SMEs are in general more inclined than large corporations to adopt non-equity-controlled forms of technology transfer and to license technology to nonaffiliate local firms.[12]

(3) *Absorptive capacities:* Perhaps the most influential factor in the success of technology transfer in developing countries is their indigenous economic and technological capability. In the absence of such indigenous capability, the absorption of imported technologies cannot take place.

Strengthening absorptive capacity requires a composite of interrelated factors.

(a) A certain threshold level of technological expertise and skilled labor is needed in order to make appropriate selections from among a range of available technologies and to modify them to local needs. Technological and scientific infrastructure should be mature enough to meet the minimum technical requirements for the type of imported technology, including such factors as sufficient supply of repair parts, raw materials, and electrical power.

(b) Political stability, institutional structure, and development banks must be improved in order to facilitate efficient management of technology transfer.

(c) R & D is crucial to expedite effective technology transfer and to improve technologies for local needs.

C.2 Human Resources Development and Entrepreneurship

As discussed in Section B, technology is embodied both in machines and equipment as tangible asset, and in people with technical and management skills as human assets. Both must be considered together for effective transfer and development of technology.

To build up technological capability, it is necessary to develop the human resources base over the entire range of engineers, technologists, and skills in macroeconomic management and policy-making in the field of technology. Indeed, suitable skills are required for identifying appropriate technology, specifying technical requirements, negotiating financial and commercial aspects of technology transactions, and assessing the economic and developmental impact of technology choices and policy options.

Table 10.4 presents indicators of investment in technology and human skills for 29 selected developing countries and territories. Countries with high levels of capital stock and technology inflow tend to have high levels of educational training and research and development expenditure, displaying a systematic, though not consistent pattern.

In terms of educational enrollment in science and technology per 100,000 population, the highest ratios, in ascending order, are in Singapore, the Republic of Korea, the Philippines, and Taiwan in the range from 704 to 795. Taiwan has a reputation for coherent adjustment in policies and measures in human resource development in accordance with the requirements of different stages of economic development. Educational training policy has gradually shifted from technical and vocational education to development of scientific and technological talent as the economy transited from labor-intensive manufacturing to the development of scientific and technological talent.[13] In terms of research and development expenditure as a percentage of GNP, the highest ratios, in ascending order, are in India, Singapore, Taiwan, and the Republic of Korea, ranging from 0.9 to 2.3 percent. The Republic of Korea continues to have the highest level of R & D expenditure in the developing world.

In contrast, the lack of skilled human resources does constitute a major impediment to the development of technology in least developed countries, particularly in Sub-Saharan Africa. It appears from Table 10.4 that enrollment in secondary education as a ratio of age group, for instance, is as low as only 4 percent in the United Republic of Tanzania. Such a low educational level would not be sufficient to provide a basis for effective transfer and development of technology.

At this point, it is worthwhile to note that mere possession of human skills is a necessary but not a sufficient condition for industrial success. As illustrated by the experience of Eastern Europe, there has long existed an ample stock of human capital and technical skills. But lack of entrepreneurship and market-based incentives, combined with institutional weakness and isolation from world technologies, led to poor industrial performance.

The main point to be emphasized here is that entrepreneurs are the link between innovation, technical progress, and production.

Table 10.4
Investment in Technology and Skills

29 developing countries and territories by region	Total capital stock[a] 1980 = 100		Technology inflows as % of GDI[b]			Human resources 1987 or closest available year				Research and development expenditure (Latest available year)	
						Literacy rate %	Educational enrollment			Total as % of GNP	Of which the productive sector as % of GNP
	1972	1988	MCG[c] 1975-87	FDI[d] 1975-87	TC[e] 1975-87		At 2nd level as % of age group	Science and technology 3rd level[f]	Vocational training 2nd level		
Côte d'Ivoire	43	73	26.2	3.6	4.0	43	18	27	249	0.3	::
Egypt	26	184	62.0	14.6	6.4	44	69	167	1833	0.2	0.039
Kenya	56	103	30.2	2.1	7.3	59	21	22	25	0.8	::
Nigeria	22	74	18.2	3.4	0.3	42	29	24	98	0.3	::
Tunisia	28	133	28.4	5.6	3.0	51	40	126	1225	::	::
United Rep. of Tanzania	42	68	20.8	0.6	11.3	46	4	3	::	::	::
Zambia	78	87	42.3	7.1	8.2	76	17	18	38	0.5	::
Argentina	67	76	8.1	2.0	0.1	94	74	363	3834	0.4	0.179
Brazil	35	100	8.7	3.5	0.1	78	38	160	1092	0.4	0.268
Chile	96	88	21.5	3.8	0.9	91	70	538	1062	0.5	0.211
Colombia	56	119	20.4	9.5	0.9	85	56	387	1515	0.1	0.002
Costa Rica	49	92	20.9	6.9	3.4	93	41	312	981	0.3	0.000
Ecuador	29	101	26.3	2.8	4.6	80	56	636	2624	0.5	::
Guatemala	55	64	18.1	8.1	2.4	46	20	::	430	0.6	::
Mexico	61	111	21.0	3.5	0.1	90	53	453	1051	0.6	0.173
Peru	54	78	17.3	0.2	1.7	82	65	563	297	0.2	::
Uruguay	69	74	13.2	0.4	1.0	95	73	379	1359	0.2	::
Venezuela	38	96	22.6	0.6	0.1	85	54	558	304	0.3	::

Table 10.4
Investment in Technology and Skills (Continued)

29 developing countries and territories by region	Total capital stock[a] 1980 = 100		Technology Inflows as % of GDI[b]			Human resources 1987 or closest available year					Research and development expenditure (Latest available year)	
						Educational enrollment						Of which the productive sector as % of GNP
	1972	1988	MCG[c] 1975-87	FDI[d] 1975-87	TC[e] 1975-87	Literacy rate %	At 2nd level as % of age group	Science and technology 3rd level[f]	Vocational training 2nd level		Total as % of GNP	
Hong Kong	..	..	39.0	7.0	0.1	77	72	318	800		..	..
India	63	165	8.6	0.2	0.4	41	35	..	80		0.9	0.191
Indonesia	26	177	17.2	1.5	1.1	67	39	16	626		0.3	..
Malaysia	33	167	34.9	9.0	0.8	70	59	85	122		..	..
Pakistan	80	165	20.4	1.3	2.4	26	18	28	51		0.4	0.327
Philippines	62	71	29.3	1.5	1.1	83	64	770			0.1	0.023
Rep. of Korea	21	239	25.7	0.9	0.1	88	89	765	1970		2.3	1.543
Singapore	25	169	88.4	16.8	0.3	83	69	704	372		0.9	0.521
Taiwan Prov. of China	..	..	33.2	3.3	..	92	91	795	2082		1.1	0.738
Thailand	49	147	23.6	3.0	1.4	79	30	..	648		0.3	..
Turkey	44	156	25.0	0.8	0.5	74	46	222	1402		0.7	0.532

Source: UNCTAD secretariat computations based on data from UNIDO, UNSO, UNCTC, OECD and UNESCO. Table source: United Nations, *Transfer and Development of Technology in a Changing World Environment: The Challenges of the 1990s,* United Nations publication, Sales No. TD/C.6/156 (1991), p. 21.

a See figure 1 for the calculation of capital stocks
b Gross domestic investment
c Capital goods imports.
d Foreign direct investment.
e Technical co-operation grants.
f Third-level students in natural science, mathematics and computer science, engineering, and transport and communications.

C.3   Government Policies and Measures

Transfer and development of technology cannot operate in a vacuum. One of the clearest lessons of the Japanese and East Asian experience on effective transfer and development of technology is the role played by a strategy and its associated policies for importing established technology from abroad. There is an urgent need for every country to set up science and technology policies to address specific objectives, in particular in the areas of the development of indigenous technology, sectoral priorities for development, provision of supporting infrastructure, and selection, acquisition, adaptation, and improvement of imported technologies. Although laws and regulations have been established by many countries on an ad hoc basis in various areas, such as foreign investment, science planning, and intellectual property, it is only in the past decade that technology has been given attention by policymakers as a subject in its own right.

Policy actions require attention by both recipient countries and the international community. First, on policy actions to be taken by recipient countries, Table 10.5 presents three main categories of policy instruments. Some deal specifically with the encouragement of technological innovation and the promotion of transfer of technology such as investment in R & D. Others deal with general economic measures having an indirect impact on technology decisions, such as trade, monetary, and labor force policies.

The three main categories of policy instruments of active technology transfer as presented in Table 10.5 are highlighted next:

(a)   *Macroeconomic policy framework:* Macroeconomic framework affects the pace and choice of technology transfer through its effects on many areas such as foreign and domestic investment, trade, and financial resources. These policies are designed to foster the free operation of market forces for externalized technology transfer. These macroeconomic policies have to be mutually consistent with the broader development strategy and macroeconomic policy framework, especially in relation to industrial development and import policies. Many policies are interrelated, thus requiring a responsible agency to coordinate implementation. As illustrated earlier, the MITI of Japan coordinates government policies for foreign investment, industrial development and technology transfer with the result that Japanese enterprises can exercise considerable bargaining power in negotiations with technology suppliers.

(b)   *Regulation of technology imports:* There is considerable evidence that technology markets can operate to the disadvantage of recipient countries, with regard to both price charges for access to technology and terms and conditions attached to its use. Thus, most countries have enacted legislative provisions or administrative guidelines on the terms of the contract for technology transfer among suppliers, recipients, and governments. It covers a wide range of areas, such as foreign exchange

Table 10.5

Main Categories of Policy Instruments for Active Technology Transfer

A. MACRO-ECONOMIC POLICY FRAMEWORK

    (i)   Characteristics of development strategy and policies
    (ii)   Foreign investment policies
    (iii) Industrial development policies
    (iv) Import policies
    (v)   Fiscal, monetary and credit policies
    (vi) Public investment program and policies

B. REGULATION OF TECHNOLOGY IMPORTS

"Negative" **approval standards**

    (i)   Payment terms
    (ii)   Restrictive practices in contracts
    (iii) Duration of contracts
    (iv) Domestic availability of technology

"Positive" **approval standards**

    (i)   Collection of information on availability of technology
    (ii)   Search, selection and negotiation/bargaining procedures
    (iii) Personnel training
    (iv) Research and development activities

C. PROMOTION OF LOCAL TECHNOLOGY

    (i)   National science and technology planning
    (ii)   Education and training of technological manpower
    (iii) Investment in research and development
    (iv) Support for the engineering and capital goods sectors
    (v)   Provision of technology information systems

Source: United Nations, *United Nations Guidelines for Development Planning,* United Nations publication, Sales No. E.87.II.H.1 (1987), p. 54.

outflows, protection of infant industries, and safe transfer of technology to prevent industrial accidents such as the one that occurred in Bhopal, India, in 1984. Many policies deal with encouragement of technology absorption and development, such as mandates on the training of the recipient country's personnel in production, management, and higher technology and on the arrangements for research and development and engineering design by suppliers.

(c)   *Promotion of local technology:* Japan's policies in the 1950s and 1960s served as a model for many developing countries in their insistence that technology transfer must contribute to local development. The Foreign Investment Act of 1950 in Japan together with other policy measures was designed to strengthen the role of government in requiring that the acquisition of foreign technology should contribute to the establishment of new industries with a view to reducing the country's dependence on foreign technology. The public sector should provide important research and other infrastructure services facilities for Japanese industries, and the government would serve as a watchdog over technology transfer to secure Japan's best long-term interests. Many developing countries adopted Japan's approach in the 1970s and 1980s. Countries like mainland China and Poland have also introduced similar policies. In this regard, most developing countries have adopted policy measures to intensify efforts to promote education, develop infrastructure, enhance domestic R & D, and integrate technology into the mainstream of macroeconomic planning.

Second, on policy actions to be taken by the international community, a common theme is that such measures should be conducive to the mutual interest of both developed and developing countries in promoting the increase of international technology flow. International cooperation has paid particular attention to the following two areas:

(a)   The prevailing concern over the International Code of Conduct on the Transfer of Technology and protection of intellectual property should not be considered in isolation, but in relation to the promotion of technology transfer and the development objectives of developing countries. The developed countries have dominated technological innovation in the world economy. In particular, new technology of informatics, semiconductors, new materials, and biotechnology which were developed through high technology with high costs is prohibitively expensive for developing countries. Developing countries have remained dependent on imported technology because of their weak industrial base. Although there is a need to safeguard the legitimate rights and interests of suppliers, this should not result in an adverse effect on technology transfer to developing countries. In this regard, many developing countries have adopted legislative measures on joint ventures and on favorable terms of agreement in attracting foreign investment.

(b)   In order to revitalize technology flows to developing countries, decisive steps must be taken by the international community to ease the adverse effects of excessive debt, balance-of-payments constraints, and weak export commodity prices of economically stricken countries, especially in Africa and Latin America. Also, developed countries could encourage technology transfer to developing countries through such policy measures as concessional credit and tax incentives (e.g., greater responsibility for offsetting losses on investment in developing countries against home-country tax liabilities). Furthermore, international agencies and donor countries could further strengthen noncommercial forms of technical assistance to developing countries through provision of technical experts and training of engineers and R & D personnel.

D. REMARKS ON INDUSTRIAL PARKS

Establishment of industrial parks has been listed among governments' top priorities in their effort to promote industrial development. Generally speaking, industrial parks are affiliated, formally or informally, with universities and research institutes and are dedicated to science and technology for products and manufacturing. However, there are other types of industrial parks dedicated to basic and applied research without extensive manufacturing activities, or to organized production activities for export through the use of local labor, the so-called export zone.

In the United States, the most successful and well-known example is the Silicon Valley with its reputation of rapid growth in high-tech industry. Other industrial parks could not match the scale of success achieved by the Silicon Valley. For example, in the Research Triangle of North Carolina, located near three excellent universities and receiving strong support from public funds between 1981 and 1990, only three electronics companies had reached the stage of having their stocks available for initial public offering, a sign of success of start-up companies, in contrast to 128 companies in the Silicon Valley during the same period. The slow growth of the Research Triangle of North Carolina may be attributed to such factors as the conservative culture in the area, lack of management talent, and changes of government priorities.

In Taiwan, the Hsinchu Science-Based Industrial Park was established by the government in 1980. The park is located near the two best known universities in science education and research. The number of companies had grown to 103 in this industrial park by 1989. It is expected to double in size and work force by 1996 with a total revenue of over US$8 billion, and to account for 10 percent of the domestic industrial turnover. It has attracted many overseas Chinese professionals, who have gained practical experience in high-tech companies in developed countries, particularly in the United States, to serve as entrepreneurs. This is one of the most successful examples of a high-tech park in Asia. Its success can be attributed to the government's effort to ensure continuous financing and highly efficient management.

At this point, it is worthwhile to cite the role of the Industrial Technology Research Institute (ITRI) in promoting industrial development in Taiwan, which is located in Hsinchu Science-Based Industrial Park. Several unique features of ITRI relate to its contribution to Taiwan's industrial development.

(a)   It is a government-funded institute with a total budget of about US$360 million in 1992. For maximum flexibility and effectiveness, ITRI was chartered as a private organization. It carries out long-term and medium-term applied research in line with government development strategies for promoting high-tech industries. The results of its research are transferred to the industrial sector on a nonexclusive basis under the principles of fairness and openness. In fiscal year 1991, various technologies obtained from 74 projects were transferred to 102 companies.

(b)   ITRI directly participated in the technological development of the industrial sector through contract research and provision of technical advice. In 1992, ITRI received more than US$100 million from the industrial sector. In line with government development objectives, ITRI provides technical assistance to small and medium-size industries as well as major state-owned enterprises.

(c)   ITRI has provided a career transition base to the industrial sector for professionals. In particular, many overseas professionals were first attracted to join ITRI and then were attracted to the industrial sector. It is estimated that over 3,000 former ITRI employees now work in local industries in various capacities, ranging from production manager, to manager of research and development, to chief executive. This is another aspect of ITRI's contribution to Taiwan's industrial development through its transfer of competent professionals.

NOTES

1. Major references for the preparation of this chapter are several United Nations publications: United Nations, *Transfer and Development of Technology in a Changing World Environment: The Challenges of the 1990s,* prepared by the United Nations Conference on Trade and Development (UNCTAD), TD/B/C.6/153 (1991); United Nations, *Report of the Committee on Transfer of Technology,* prepared by UNCTAD, TD/B/1203 (1989); United Nations, *Technology Policies for Development and Selected Issues for Action,* Proceedings of a seminar organized by Islamic Development Bank and UNCTAD, United Nations publication Sales No. E.88.II.A.4 (1988).

2. According to a recent study of the Group of Five countries of France, West Germany, Japan, the United Kingdom, and the United States, technical progress accounts for more

than 50 percent of economic growth, followed by the growth of capital input. Together the two factors account for more than 75 percent of the growth of real output in the Group of Five countries. The remaining 25 percent is attributed to labor. The methodology adopted is a modification of the metaproduction function. Data used are from 1957 to 1985 except for West Germany and the United States, data for which began in 1960 and 1948, respectively. See Michael J. Boskin and Lawrence J. Lau, "Post-War Economic Growth in the Group-of-Five Countries: A New Analysis," Center for Economic Policy Research, Stanford University, publication no. 217, Palo Alto, Calif.: CEPR, 1990.

3. Although there is some degree of overlap, the main forms of technology transfers can be classified into the following categories: (1) foreign direct investment, (2) joint ventures, (3) licensing, (4) franchising, (5) management contracts, (6) marketing contracts, (7) technical service contracts, (8) turnkey contracts, and (9) international subcontracts.

For further discussion of the definition of these categories, determinants of the form of technology transfer and its effectiveness, and the costs of alternative forms see United Nations, *Trade and Development Report 1987,* prepared by UNCTAD, United Nations publication Sales No. E.87.II.D.7 (1987), chapters 1-3.

4. The period of the 1960s was characterized by a rapid increase in the flow of capital goods related to technology transfer. The United States was responsible for an average of 30 percent of the world outflows of foreign direct investments because of its rapid expansion of firms abroad, particularly in Western Europe. During the period from 1973 until late 1970s, technology-related flow registered a continuing higher growth than during the 1960s (but slower growth, if expressed in real terms). Exports of capital goods to the developing countries also continued to expand strongly.

For a detailed analysis of the dimension, growth, and direction of technology flows in the 1960s, 1970s, and early 1980s see United Nations, *Trade and Development Report 1987,* pp. 86-92. For an analysis of this subject during the period of the 1980s see United Nations, *Transfer and Development,* chapter 1.

5. Several individual countries deviated from this pattern of decreasing technology transfer in this grouping average of developing countries. In addition to several newly industrializing economies in Eastern Asia, mainland China, for instance, has had a significant increase in the flow of direct investment since 1979. These inflows are estimated to have been about US$4 billion in the period 1980-1985. See United Nations, *Trade and Development Report 1987,* p. 91.

6. For instance, the preferential trading arrangements between its six ASEAN members: Malaysia, Indonesia, the Philippines, Singapore, Thailand, and Brunei cover an impressive number of 15,752 items. But according to a report by Singapore, they account for less than 1 percent of members' external trade. See *The Economist,* 9-15 March 1991 (London), p. 36.

7. A report prepared by the UNCTC (United Nations, *Trade and Development Report 1987,* p. 34) discusses six aspects of the development of capabilities to achieve effective technology transfer:

(a) Search and consciously select the most relevant imported technology for a particular purpose;

(b) Negotiate and acquire imported technology on the best possible terms (financial and otherwise);

(c) Assimilate imported technology to the point where the production system installed (plant, processes, and equipment) can be operated, maintained, and repaired without foreign assistance;

(d) Modify, adapt, and improve imported technology;

(e) Replicate imported technology, using domestic design and engineering skills and domestic manufacturing facilities;

(f) Develop new technologies and new production systems based on them, using domestic skills and facilities.

8. The Japanese experience cannot be easily replicated by many developing countries because they lack Japan's economic and cultural infrastructure and a large domestic market. Nonetheless, the Japanese experience contains some lessons of interest to developing countries in their search for effective transfer and development of technology.

9. The Republic of Korea has been frequently cited as a good model among developing countries in the diffusion of new techniques to the local economy. A survey of 112 exporting firms in 1976 found that both foreign and domestic firms exhibited a high rate of innovation in the introduction of new products. Many of the innovations introduced by both foreign and domestic firms were subsequently copied by local firms. See L. E. Westphal, Y. W. Rhee, and G. Pursell, "Korean Industrial Competence: Where It Came From," World Bank Staff Working Paper No. 0469 (Washington, D.C., 1981), pp. 32-35.

10. See Linsu Kim, "Entrepreneurship and Innovation in a Rapidly Developing Country," in United Nations, *Journal of Development Planning No. 18 on Entrepreneurship and Economic Development,* United Nations publication Sales No. E.88.II.A.13 (1988), p. 184.

11. See Emil Herbolzheimer and Habib Ouane, "The Transfer of Technology to Developing Countries by Small and Medium-Sized Enterprises of Developed Countries," in United Nations, *Trade and Development – An UNCTAD Review,* No. 6, United Nations publication Sales No. E.85.II.D.20 (1985), p. 133.

12. Ibid., p. 142.

13. See K. T. Li, "The Development of Human Resources," *Industry of Free China,* no. 3 (1991) pp. 47-53.

BIBLIOGRAPHY

Agarwala, Ramgopal. "Planning in Developing Countries, Lessons of Experience." *World Bank Staff Working Papers,* No. 576, Washington, D.C., 1989.

Bhouraskar, D. M. "Financing Privatization: Role of Government." Paper prepared for a United Nations project, Transnational Corporations and Management Division. New York, May 1992.

Borgatti, Joseph J. "Method of Privatization of State-Owned Enterprises." Paper prepared for a United Nations project, Transnational Corporations and Management Division, New York, May 1992.

Boskin, Michael J., and Lau, Laurence J. "Post-War Economic Growth in the Group-of-Five Countries: A New Analysis." Center for Economic Policy Research, Stanford University, Publication No. 217. Palo Alto, Calif.: CEPR, 1990.

Economist, London, 9-15 March 1991.

Herbolzheimer, Emil, and Ouane, Habib. "The Transfer of Technology to Developing Countries by Small and Medium-Sized Enterprises of Developed Countries." *Trade and Development – An UNCTAD Review,* No. 6. United Nations publication Sales No. E.85.II.D.20, New York, 1985.

International Monetary Fund. *World Economic Outlook.* Washington, D.C., April 1989.

Kim, Linsu. "Entrepreneurship and Innovation in a Rapidly Developing Country." *Journal of Development Planning,* No. 18. United Nations publication Sales No. E.88.II.A.13, New York, 1988.

Leibenstein, Harvey, and Roy, Dennis, guest editors. "Entrepreneurship and Economic Development." *Journal of Development Planning,* no. 18. United Nations publication Sales No. E.88.II.A.13, New York, 1988.

Lewis, W. Arthur. *The Theory of Economic Growth.* Homewood, Ill.: George Allen and Irwin, 1955.

Li, K. T. "The Development of Human Resources." *Industry of Free China.* LXXV, no. 3, (1991).

Li, K. T. *The Evolution of Policy Behind Taiwan's Development Success.* New Haven, Conn.: Yale University Press, 1988.

Lin, Wuu-Long. "Trend and Structural Changes in the Financial Resources of the Public Sector with Special Focus on Developing Countries," *The Role of Public Sec-*

tor in Promoting the Economic Development of Developing Countries, United Nations, DDSMS/SEM. 94/2, New York, 1994.

Little, Ian M. D. "An Economic Reconnaissance." *Economic Growth and Structural Change in Taiwan,* ed. by Walter Galenson, Ithaca, N.Y.: Cornell University Press, 1979.

Organization for Economic Cooperation and Development. *The Evaluation of Technical Assistance.* Paris, 1969.

Please, Stanley. "Saving Through Taxation: Reality or Mirage?" *Finance and Development.* 4, no. 1, 1967.

Please, Stanley. "The 'Please Effect' Revisited." *World Bank Working Paper,* no. 82, 1970.

Prest, A. R. *Public Finance in Developing Countries,* 3rd edition, New York: St. Martin's Press, 1985.

Prokopenko, Joseph, and Pavlin, Igor, editors. *Entrepeneurship Development in Public Enterprises.* Management Development Series no. 29, International Labour Office, Geneva, 1991.

Saunders, Peter, and Klau, Friedrich. *The Role of the Public Sector.* OECD Economics Studies no. 4, Paris, 1985.

Small and Medium Enterprise Agency, Ministry of International Trade and Industry. *Small Business in Japan 1991: White Paper on Small and Medium Enterprise in Japan.* Tokyo, Japan 1991.

Stolper, Wolfgang F. *Planning Without Facts; Lessons in Resource Allocation from Nigeria's Development.* Cambridge, Mass.: Harvard University Press, 1966.

Tinbergen, Jan. *The Design of Development.* Baltimore: The Johns Hopkins University Press, 1958.

United Nations. *Accrual Accounting in Developing Countries.* United Nations publication Sales No. E.84.II.H.2, New York, 1984.

United Nations. *Government Financial Management in Least Developed Countries.* United Nations publication Sales No. E.91.II.H.1, New York, 1991.

United Nations. *Guidelines for Development Planning.* United Nations publication Sales No. E.87.II.H.1, New York, 1987.

United Nations. *Planning and Control of Public Current Expenditure – Lessons of Country Experience.* United Nations publication Sales No. E.87.II.H.3, New York, 1987.

United Nations. *Report of the Ad Hoc Committee of the Whole for the Preparation of the International Development Strategy for the Fourth United Nations Development Decade.* General Assembly Supplement No. 41 (A/45/41), New York, 1991.

United Nations. *Report of the Committee on Transfer of Technology.* By United Nations Conference on Trade and Development (UNCTAD). United Nations publication Sales No. TD/B/1203, New York, 1988.

United Nations. *Role and Extent of Competition in Improving the Performance of Public Enterprises.* TDC/Sem.89/2, INT-88-R59, New York, 1989.

United Nations. *Technology Policies for Development and Selected Issues for Action.* Proceedings of a seminar organized by Islamic Development Bank and UNCTAD. United Nations publication, Sales No. E.88.II.A.4, New York, 1988.

United Nations. "The Evolution of the External Debt Problem in Latin America and in the Caribbean." *Estudios e Informes de la CEPAL,* No. 72. United Nations publication Sales No. E.88.II.G.10, 1988.

United Nations. *Trade and Development Report.* By United Nations Conference on Trade and Development (UNCTAD). United Nations E.87.II.D.7, New York, 1987.

United Nations. *Transfer and Development of Technology in a Changing World Environment: The Challenges of the 1990s.* By United Nations Conference on Trade and Development (UNCTAD). United Nations, TD/B/C.6/156, New York, 1991.

United Nations. *Transnational Corporations in World Development: Trends and Prospects.* United Nations publication Sales No. E.88.II.A.7, New York, 1988.

United Nations. *World Economic Survey 1989.* United Nations publication Sales No. E.89.II.C.1, New York, 1989.

United Nations. *World Population Trends and Policies.* United Nations publication Sales No. E.82.XIII.2, New York, 1982.

United States General Accounting Office. *Managing the Cost of Government, Building an Effective Financial Management Structure.* GAO/Afmd-85-35-A, Washington, D.C., 1985.

World Bank. *Sub-Saharan Africa: From Crisis to Sustainable Growth.* New York: Oxford University Press, 1989.

World Bank. *World Development Report 1980.* New York: Oxford University Press, 1980.

World Bank. *World Development Report 1983.* New York: Oxford University Press, 1983.

World Bank. *World Development Report 1985.* New York: Oxford University Press, 1985.

World Bank. *World Development Report 1987.* New York: Oxford University Press, 1987.

World Bank. *World Development Report 1988.* New York: Oxford University Press, 1988.

World Bank. *World Development Report 1989.* New York: Oxford University Press, 1989.

World Bank. *World Development Report 1991.* New York: Oxford University Press, 1991.

World Bank. *World Development Report 1992.* New York: Oxford University Press, 1992.

Waterston, Albert. *Development Planning: Lessons of Experience.* Baltimore: The Johns Hopkins University Press, 1982.

Westphal, L. E., Rhee, Y. W., and Pursell, G. "Korean Industrial Competence: Where It Came From." *World Bank Staff Working Paper,* no. 0469. Washington, D.C., July 1981.

Wright, Maurice. "Public Expenditure in Britain: The Crises of Control." *Public Administration,* 55, Summer 1977.

INDEX

About the Authors

WUU-LONG LIN is currently Senior Economic Affairs Officer and former Chief, Enterprise Management of the United Nations, and Adjunct Econometric Professor of Baruch College, School of Business, City University of New York. He has served the United Nations for twenty years and has traveled to approximately thirty developing countries to provide technical advice on development planning, public finance, and enterprise management. He is the author of seven books and pamphlets.

THOMAS P. CHEN is Associate Professor of Economics and Finance at St. John's University, New York. He specializes in economic development, international trade, economic forcasting, and technological changes. He has lectured in Taiwan and China, and has served as a consultant to various international agencies.

ISBN 0-275-94819-6

90000>

EAN

9 780275 948191

HARDCOVER BAR CODE